THE BEST BITS
OF
BRINSON'S COLUMN

Dave Brinson

© Dave Brinson 2010
Content first published online at davebrinson.blogspot.com 2007-9
Printed and bound by Lulu inc.

ISBN 978-0-9559803-1-2

Photo credits: *Harriet Harman, by Steve Punter, licenced under Creative Commons Attribution ShareAlike 2.0. Co-opeartive Store by Kaishu Tai, licensed under the Creative Commons Attribution ShareAlike 3.0. Peter Hain, from official US congressional picture, released into the public domain. Ed Balls, by Jarvin, under the terms of the GNU Free Documentation License, (Version 1.2). Ken Livingstone at the London Mayoral result, by secretlondon, under the terms of the GNU Free Documentation License. Gordon Brown at 2008 Labour Conference, by Adrian Scottow, licensed under Creative Commons Attribution ShareAlike 2.0. Diane Abbott at the third European Social Forum, by JK the Unwise under the terms of the GNU Free Documentation License, (Version 1.2) Ann Widdecombe, released into the public domain by its author, Manchester2k6 at the Wikipedia project. Benazir Bhutto, by I Faqeer, under the terms of the GNU Free Documentation License, Version 1.2 Zsolt Biczo. Aneurin Bevan, by Associated Press (Australia) Out of copyright. Gurkha Soldiers from The Navy and Army Illustrated 24.7.1896 (out of copyright)*

Dave speaking at NUT Teachers rally, Tim Lucas 2008. Teachers rally at Eastbourne Bandstand. Taken by the author. Dave at Brighton Pride 2007, with thanks to Lis Telcs. Primark- picture taken in Eastbourne Arndale Centre by the author. International Brigades performance- picture by Richard Goude. Ann Ring with the author and Martin Falkner at 10 Downing Street, photo by Jon Pettigrew. Photo of Dorothy Brinson, by the author. Photos of Eastbourne DGH by the Author.
Palace of Westminster- © eg114703 at Dreamstime.com. Downing Street- ©Brian Nguyen at Dreamstime.com Glasgow- © Stephen Finn at Dreamstime.com. Ballot papers- © Stuart Key at Dreamstime.com Gavel and EU flag, © Gina Saunders at Dreamstime.com. Birthday Cake- © RobinsonSky at Dreamstime.com Red Arrow- ©marbo at Dreamstime.com. Solider feet- © Pavel Losevsky at Dreamstime.com. Rail Station- © Matthew Scholey at Dreamstime.com. Working Family: © Monket Business Images at Dreamstime.com

DEDICATION

This book is dedicated to all the people in it.

To my colleagues in education, my comrades in the Eastbourne Labour Party, my political opponents who (nearly always) avoid making it personal and ensure a robust yet good natured debate, to my mother Pat, who has always supported me, and my friends who keep me smiling and swiftly warn me when I take myself too seriously.

Special thoughts to those who are no longer with us: to Len Caine, Terry Page, Ann and Brian Ring, and, of course, to Nan.

And to the "other DB"- with love.

CONTENTS

Labour Days……………………………… 6

The Opposition…………………………… 46

Health …………………………………….. 66

Education………………………………… 82

All Different, All Equal………………… 100

The Airbourne Fisaco……….……………. 108

Up the Workers!.. 116

Law and Liberty………………………….. 128

Arty Time……………………………...… 140

Transport………………………………….. 152

One World- Our World………………….. 160

The Political: The Personal……………..… 176

The articles in this book are sorted into chapters reflecting the broad themes contained within them. In most cases, the articles within each chapter follow date order, although there a few exceptions to this for layout or continuity reasons. And because I'm a bit quirky.

INTRODUCTION

I've always loved writing, and putting my thoughts down on paper, but have never cracked the art of keeping a diary. So, when I (eventually) discovered the new art of the online 'blog, I thought I'd give it a go.

"Brinson's Column" was my attempt to share thoughts about politics, education and Eastbourne with anyone out there who took an interest. Between June 2007 and January 2009, I tried to regularly write about something- some weeks were better than others.

By January 2009, my postings were becoming fewer as the work of a teacher, union official and political activist started to suck up more of my time, and I called it a day shortly after the New Year.

For about a year after that, I fleetingly came back to the question- could I really be self-important enough to try and publish it in book form ? Well, eventually, owing to the advances of digital printing and the fact that there are a few family and friends out there who don't "do" the Internet, I did.

If you are reading this, you've got hold of a copy. I hope that I might make you think- whether or not you agree with me. Perhaps I might tell you something you don't know, or don't like. Maybe you'll agree with every word?

Whatever happens- I hope you enjoy it.

DB

LABOUR DAYS

*I joined the Labour Party as an idealistic school student in 1994. Since then, I have been that rare creature in Eastbourne- a Labour Activist. From Young Labour chair, through local government candidate, chair of the constituency party and now Parliamentary Candidate, I have remained, resolutely, a Labour man- the odd disagreement or difficulty over policy notwithstanding ! It's **my** party- left or right- and this selection of columns charts my thoughts on the internal politics and policy goings-on of my Party.*

Thursday, 14 June 2007
Labour's deputy leadership

As a paid up Labour member (Chair of Eastbourne Constituency, for those that don't know me,) I cast my ballot for the Deputy leadership contest today.

Difficult choice, as there are no candidates that I would actively dislike as Deputy Leader (although one comes close, as you'll see...)

In the end, I cast my vote for Jon Cruddas. The Dagenham MP is an independent minded backbencher, who has made it clear that he would not wish to serve as Deputy PM, rather seeing his role as leading the rebuilding of the Labour Party membership and sharpening us up for the fight in 2009/10. This is exactly what we need. In my area, we couldn't muster enough candidates for every seat in the local elections- we need a real push to be ready to mount a General election campaign. Cruddas has good relations with the Trade Unions and a record of fighting the BNP.

Other votes were:

2. Hilary Benn. Principled and amiable Overseas Development Secretary, with a long history in the Party (in his own right- not just his Dad...) Good name recognition and potential unifier of activists. Also nominated by my CLP- which counts for something.

3. Peter Hain: Capable, thoughtful, with a radical past. Not totally sure where he stands as he seems to be swinging left-right on an almost daily basis. Had my #1 vote until a couple of weeks ago, though!

4. Harriet Harman: Good recognition factor, thoughtful on policy, although loses points as a formerly impeccable Blairite who's now ridiculously trying to posture Left. Gender balance would be good, but Harriet is pushing the "vote for me because I'm a woman" line in a rather unsubtle way, which could be counter-productive.

5. Hazel Blears: Good campaigner, great party roots and hard worker. My fear is that she comes over very poorly in the media- the loyal adherence to the Party line on all things can make her come across as a bit of a lightweight (unfairly) Hazel describes herself as the "Marmite Candidate" (as in "you either love her or you hate her".) Not great for a post that needs to be unifying!

6. Alan Johnson: I'm a teacher. I'd chew my own arm off first. He's pushing through the ill-conceived and grubby Academy project, and despite proclaiming his trade union credentials, has gleefully chucked the NUT and NASUWT into a cockpit and urged them to try and tear each other apart- damaging the unity of a fine profession.

Any of 1-5 would be fine- and I could probably grow to love AJ when he's freed from DfES.

Pity we didn't get a vote on the leadership. Right result: wrong way of getting it. I'd have voted for Gordon anyway, but I think we've missed a chance to give him a proper whole-membership endorsement. Also, in a constituency without Labour councillors or an MP, it was a rare chance for local members to actually have a real say in the way we're governed.

Sunday, 24 June 2007
Blimey, it's Harriet

Well, I wish I was a gambling man, as I'd have picked up a healthy few quid today, after Harriet Harman was elected as Labour Party leader. Most polls were placing her fourth, with Johnson and Benn battling it out with a stiff outside challenge from Jon Cruddas.

Harriet, though, is a true Labour survivor. She was the only candidate who had "seen action" in the 1980's, in fact only she and Peter Hain had been in Parliament under the Tory government. She's the only one who had been a front bencher in opposition, and, despite a few years in the wilderness, has good name-recognition factor.

Harriet was seen as an ultra-loyal Blairite in the early days of this government. However, in recent years she was seen as more closely aligned to the Brown camp, and has made open overtures to the Left of the Party during this campaign, especially over housing and Iraq. She was backed by both high-profile front benchers like Patricia Hewitt, Geoff Hoon and Yvette Cooper, and figures strongly associated with the Left, like Linda Riordan and Alice Mahon.

I am pleased with the result, for a number of reasons:
- As someone from the "soft-left" I welcome a deputy leader who recognises and celebrates the breadth and diversity of the Labour Party, and is not afraid of a genuine debate.
- As the wife of Jack Dromey (TGWU official) and a trade unionist in her own right, she will work constructively with the unions, and defend the role of working people's voice in the Party.
- As a former chair of the National Council for Civil Liberties (now Liberty) she clearly has a strong belief in human rights.
- As a "southerner" she will balance the team and make sure that "middle England" feels represented in the leadership.
- Finally, although she said it herself at least once too often, it is appropriate that we have a woman in a leadership role. The Labour Party has only ever had one other woman in this post in our 100+ year history, and then for less than three years. If we are serious about challenging the shameful gender-gap in political leadership in this country, it is not a bad start.

The next step, of course, is getting the Brown government together and starting to rebuild the Labour Party base to fight and win the next General

Election. Harriet will have the leading role in Party regeneration, and I look forward to being a part of it.

Eastbourne Labour Party will be having its say on what a Brown-Harman Labour Party should look like, and we'll be saying……….. well, if you're not a member, then why not sign up and be a part of it ? (he says, cheekily…)

Wednesday, 4 July 2007
Brown's first test

It has been announced that July 19th will see 2 by-elections in "safe" Labour seats: Ealing Southall and Sedgefield, with the NEC choosing to shortlist **Jo Sidhu and Virendra Sharma** in Ealing, while local son **Phil Wilson** has been selected for Tony Blair's old seat.

Phil Wilson was a great speaker at an Eastbourne Labour Party meeting a few years back- talking about the selection and career of Tony Blair in Sedgefield. He was, and presumably is, a committed "Blairite," but was prepared to debate policy and issues in a comradely way- Gill Roles and I gave him a bit of a hard time afterwards over student fees!

Ealing is a bit of a surprise, as, anticipating the retirement of the late Piara Khabra, the seat had been selected as an all-women shortlist, part of Labour's strategy to ensure more talented women MPs in Parliament. Oddly, the NEC did not apply this to the by-election selection, and have given local members the choice between two men. If the party remains committed to increasing the number of women candidates via the A.W.S, then I'm not sure that this sends out quite the right message...

Whoever the candidates are, these will be the first real test of the so-called Brown Bounce (in the polls) and may well decide whether Gordon calls an early election. The key issues will be:-

- Can Brown's leadership bring disenchanted former Labour supporters back to the party?
- Can we draw a line under policy issues that have dogged us in the last few years, such as Iraq?
- Most importantly for me- and the Labour faithful in Eastbourne, is can we defuse a "protest vote" campaign by the Lib Dems?

The Lib Dems always do well in by-elections, whatever the prevailing political wind. In the last Parliament, they took Dunfermline from Labour within just a few months of what would have been the biggest upset in years- coming within a few hundred of taking Bromley off the Tories, at a time when they were supposed to be rebuilding support! They even won Eastbourne at the height of Maggie Thatcher's unpopularity.

By elections are a chance for disenchanted voters to cast a warning shot to the leaderships of the two main parties. If Brown is really going to reverse the decline in committed Labour support, then he needs a good result in both seats. If there is a serious Lib Dem challenge, then it looks like it'll be a while- probably May 2009- before Brown goes to the country.

Either way, Brown's team need to get on with challenging not just the Tories, but also the Lib Dems, who are quite happy to get into bed with the Tories in local government (Leeds, Birmingham, Camden etc.) I look forward to us leading the way in that task in Eastbourne!

Roll on July 19th!

Wednesday 1 August 2007
Hooray for the Co-Op

On Saturday I was pleased to attend the AGM of the Sussex Co-operative Party, of which I am a member. A lot of people won't be familiar with the Co-op Party, but it is 90 years old, and has 29 MPs, (and over 350 local councillors) all of whom are also members of the Labour Party. The Co-Op Party is an independent political party, with an electoral agreement with Labour, whereby its candidates stand as joint Labour and Co-operative candidates. The highest profile Co-op MP is probably Ed Balls, former economic adviser to the Chancellor, and now Secretary of State for Children, Schools and Families.

The Co-op Party exists to promote the mutual sector as a business and economic model. In co-operatives, ownership is by a group of people with equal votes in the organisation. This could be a workers co-operative, where the staff of the business collectively own it, or, more often, a consumer co-operative where staff and customers all have a share in the business. This model is particularly suited to community businesses, where the aim is not to make profits for shareholders, but to run efficiently and put the profits back into the growth of the enterprise.

The Co-op group (that runs the shops, bank, insurance, funeral directors etc.) is Britain's biggest and most successful co-operative. Hundreds of thousands of customers have paid £1 for their share in the company, have the right to elect the boards of the organisation, and receive a small cash dividend based on the amount that they use the company. Every shareholder has equal say, and (in the case of the Co-operative Group) the amount of the dividend is based on the volume of their custom, rather than how much money they have in the firm.

Building Societies such as Nationwide are a type of co-operative ("Mutual Society") credit unions are, which give people on lower incomes access to mall loans, and most working men's clubs and similar are too ("Industrial and Provident Society") A number of housing co-operatives exist- in the USA a co-operative model is very common in the way tenants of blocks of flats own and manage the freehold.

Co-operative ownership doesn't suit every business, by any means. But it is a model that has worked very well across the country in community enterprises, and, increasingly as a more efficient business model for services previously in the hands of local authorities.

How about this for a new direction for our publicly owned bus company in Eastbourne ? At the moment the "public" ownership begins and ends with the Borough Council electing four of its members to the board. The only accountability to the passengers and staff comes when they are up for re-election to the Council, and transport issues are usually overshadowed by the hot political topic of the day.

Transferring the council's shareholding (actually, the people of Eastbourne's shareholding !) to a mutual society would allow everybody who uses the service to take a stake in the company and elect directors to the board based on their expertise, skill and commitment to the success of the company and the quality of the service. It might also stop the periodic speculation about Eastbourne Borough flogging off the service to the private sector. Probably a legal minefield to set up (and would councillors want to give up another perk?) but it's nice to dream....

Wednesday, 1 August 2007
Dave declares

Having umm-ed and aah-ed for a while, I have decided to throw my hat into the ring to be Labour's prospective parliamentary candidate for Eastbourne. It now falls to my erstwhile colleagues in Eastbourne Labour Party to decide whether they want me or not....

It's the best part of a year ago that I went through the selection ("vetting") process for Labour's National Parliamentary Panel- the list of pre-approved candidates for Labour. I came out approved and relatively unscathed (although they spotted a hole in the seam of my trousers that had developed on the train journey to Reading !) The NPP isn't quite as glamorous as the Tories "A-List," but does mean that I'm considered safe enough to put on a public platform !

Eastbourne isn't a top target for the Labour Party nationally, I'll be honest. Our vote share here is in the 10-15% region (with a huge "tactical vote" squeeze from the Liberal Democrats.) But I am offering to be the candidate for a number of reasons:
- With a Labour government, everybody should have the opportunity to vote Labour in a national election. The Lib Dems are an opposition party who have voted against much of the government's policies over the last 10 years.
- The Lib Dems opposed the Minimum Wage for many years- Ming Campbell did this publicly on Question Time in 1992. They have some very right-wing MP's including those who wish to abolish the NHS and go to an insurance system with private hospitals etc.
- The Lib Dems are in coalition with the Tories on many local councils- especially in traditional Labour areas such as Birmingham, Leeds and Camden. How can we be sure that they won't do the same with "Call-me-Dave" Cameron if there is a hung parliament?
- Labour remains the friend of the trade union movement and supports the organisation of working people in modern, moderate trade unions. The Tories and Lib Dems are opposed and lukewarm respectively.
- I despise much of what Nigel Waterson MP stands for, and would like an opportunity to robustly challenge him on his policies. He needs to be taken on four-square, rather than face a wet challenge from the Lib Dem middle-ground.

As I say, it's now in the hands of the Labour Party membership in Eastbourne. Members and affiliated bodies (such as the co-op and some local trade unions) can nominate for the shortlist, and then the candidate will be chosen by a one-member-one-vote ballot of paid up members in Eastbourne.

We'll know- one way or the other- in September.

With Ann Ring and Martin Falkner at 10 Downing Street.

Saturday 8 September 2007
The campaign starts here

Last Thursday, I was privileged to be selected as the prospective Labour Party candidate to fight the Eastbourne Constituency at the next General Election. After 14 years in the Labour Party and a number of local election campaigns, I feel ready for this new challenge, and I'm deeply honoured that local Labour members believe that I'm up to the job!

With Labour finishing in third place in recent General Elections in Eastbourne, I'm bound to be asked "what's the point?" Well, as I stated in my post on August 1st, there are a number of reasons:

Labour has been in power for over 10 years, and delivered many positive changes. People have the right to express their support for our record, and vote for the party of government. Both the Tories and Lib Dems have voted against most of the government's policies over that period.
In a pluralist democracy, Eastbourne needs an active and campaigning Labour Party. Our democracy is stronger because of the range of different political points of view that are offered. The people of Eastbourne deserve to have a real choice of policies, rather than the negative "vote for us because we're not the Tories" platform that forms a centrepiece of local Lib Dem campaigning.

The Lib Dems are not a robust enough challenge to our sitting MP, Nigel Waterson. He will attack the Government's record, and the Lib Dems will, at least partially, agree with him. Waterson needs to have his policies challenged against the actual record of the Labour Government, not just against a Lib Dem manifesto that will never be tested in Westminster.
I'm also looking forward to entering the campaign as a local candidate. I have lived in Eastbourne since 1983 when I was just 5 years old. I attended local schools and college, did my student summer jobs on our glorious seafront, have been treated in the DGH, regularly travelled (and still do) on Eastbourne Buses, and know many people in our town as an individual rather than as a politician. I've been here longer than Stephen Lloyd or, indeed, our current local MP and want to get stuck in to campaigning for the future of our town.

Whether Gordon calls a snap election (hope not- give me a moment to settle in !), whether we go next spring, or indeed at any time in the next two and a half years, I'm looking forward to it immensely !

Wednesday, 27 June 2007
Very, very NEW Labour

Quentin Davies used to be a dyed-in-the-wool Thatcherite. A hang-em and flog-em Tory, he celebrated the decline of the trade unions, called the minimum wage " a crazy idea that would cause higher inflation and higher unemployment," voted against the ban on foxhunting, and against every piece of equality legislation for lesbians and gay men. [1] **Yesterday, he crossed the floor and became a Labour MP.**

Do we want this man in our party? Gut feeling tells me no. But, on the other hand, there is the real possibility that he has mellowed in his old age, and (maybe !) we have persuaded him with the success of our arguments. Alan Howarth defected in the mid 1990's, and Sean Woodward, only elected as a Tory MP in 1997, having served as one of John Major's campaign staff, defected in 1999. Both served with distinction as Labour front benchers.

Anyone can join the Labour Party- there is no interview or belief-check to allow them through. So, if an individual seeks to join the party, would it be sensible to bar him from sitting as a Labour MP? His defection has clearly done huge damage to David Cameron, and boosted the Labour Party's home on the Centre ground.

In order to decide whether to open my arms to my new comrade, a few points need clarifying:-

1. Is QD prepared to support the **policy** of the Labour Party, not just when whipped but also in the wider media (would require a fairly substantial conversion!)
2. Is he going to moderate his **homophobia**- with particular reference to the Equal Opportunities rules of the Labour Party?
3. Is he going to join an appropriate **Trade Union** (Howarth and Woodward did.)
4. Most importantly, is he going to be required to face a **selection** by Labour members if he wishes to fight the next election as a Labour candidate? (again, both Woodward and Howarth did.)

I think we were right to capitalise on his defection, and it would have been ridiculous to say we wouldn't have him, but we are right to be suspicious, and it is right that he has to do some serious political legwork before he is fully accepted. It will be interesting to see what happens.

Sunday, 23 September 2007
Time to go ?

Gordon Brown is still being evasive on the question of an early election. In an interview today with the Beeb's Andrew Marr, he brushed aside the question of an October election, saying:

"There's been speculation all the time but I think people know that over these summer months I just got on with the job." [2]

Certainly many people within the Labour Party think that we should go to the country now, with poll ratings high, and apparently undamaged by the Northern Rock crisis. Historians of the Party recall Jim Callaghan teasing the 1978 Labour Conference, and not calling the early election that he may well have won. The ensuing "Winter of Discontent" and the end of nationalist support following the rejection of devolution in a referendum sealed his fate, and ushered in 11 years of Thatcherism.

Is Brown in the same position ? What lies ahead in the next two years ? (he could actually wait until May 2010 if needs be.)

There has been an undercurrent of opinion since before the end of the Blair era that Brown should call an early General Election, as, until he did so he would not have a "democratic mandate" of his own. This, of course, is nonsense. The British electoral system places the Prime Minister as "first among equals", a leader representing the majority of elected MPs. We don't vote for a Prime Minister- we vote for an MP and they have the ultimate power to choose, and remove, the leader. Very few people are fans of the Presidential system that would be the alternative to this.

John Major, Jim Callaghan, Alec Douglas-Home and Harold Macmillan all became Prime Minister without leading their party into the previous General Election. Even Winston Churchill falls into that category- he actually didn't lead the Tories to an election victory until 1951- having lost 2 in the intervening period. The arguable difference between Brown and these others, is that everybody was expecting Brown to take over at some point during this session. To argue that the electorate was surprised at a Brown premiership is an interesting distortion of the facts.

There are some who would love for Gordon to announce a General Election in tomorrow's speech. Poll ratings suggest we could actually gain seats, and it would completely scupper the Tory Party conference, as they would probably have to cancel (the campaign would be underway, and TV reporting restrictions would be in place.) That said, it would look like a below-the-belt attack on the Tories, and would make a mockery of the earlier proposal to devolve the power to call an election to Members of Parliament.

It would also be a real strain on many Constituency Labour Parties. Most, certainly mine, are strapped for cash, and are only just embarking on the increased fundraising drive that comes in anticipation of an election campaign. To go unexpectedly would be relying on an awful lot of cheque books being opened. Not to mention the number of constituencies that have not yet selected candidates. Either they would have to rush things, or the NEC would simply impose candidates in those areas- possibly against the wishes of local activists. Not a great way of motivating supporters to go out and campaign !

The smart money has to remain on Spring 2008. This would give us time to plan and fundraise, and there is no reason to suspect that the polls will radically alter in the meantime (unless Gordon knows something we don't!) With the Tories "green group" proposing charges in supermarket car parks, there's no shortage of material for us to work with !

Tempting though the polls may be, for Brown to go now would risk earning him the dubious position in the history books as being the shortest serving Prime Minister since universal suffrage. Not an achievement for the longest serving modern chancellor to aspire to !

Sunday 7 October 2007
Solid policy from Gordon

Work commitments mean that I was unable to take advantage of my ex-officio pass to Labour Party conference last week (they will keep holding them in term time !). Fortunately, our intrepid Constituency Secretary, Richard Goude was there representing Eastbourne- his report appears in the Eastbourne Herald of 5th October .

It is not a particularly inspiring news story to state that Gordon Brown got a hugely warm reception from Labour conference- that is, these days, taken as read. But, as the leader's speech has often been rhetoric heavy and policy light (across all parties, in recent years) I was impressed by the amount of solid policy proposals that were introduced in Gordon's speech.

I am going to break the habit of a lifetime, and let someone else write the majority of this column…. with my ten favourite policy announcements from Gordon Brown's speech to Conference. Enjoy!

"one-to-one tuition will be there in our schools … for 300,000 children in English and 300,000 in maths… for every secondary pupil a personal tutor throughout their school years - and, starting with 600,000 pupils, small group tuition too."

"we want to unlock all the potential, not just the three R's, for every pupil... we aim for the first time for five hours a week sport and time for arts and music too."

"No discrimination on the basis of race, gender, sexuality, age, or faith. And no discrimination against the disabled."

"To honour those who raised us, I can affirm our commitment to restore the link between the Basic State Pension and earnings."

"We will again raise the National Minimum Wage to £5.52 an hour and …the minimum wage will be enforced without exception."

"Next week for the first time on top of holiday entitlement 4 days paid public holidays guaranteed."

"We plan to help first time buyers and we will increase house-building to 240,000 new homes a year - in places and ways that respect our green spaces and the environment. My aim by 2010: two million more homeowners than in 1997."

"We will use unclaimed assets in dormant bank accounts to build new youth centres, and we will invest over £670 million pounds so that in every community there are places for young people to go. With youth budgets let us say to young people: for the first time you will have a say over how the money is spent"

"We will more than double the number of hospital matrons to 5,000. We will give matrons and ward sisters in all 10,000 wards the powers to report cleaning contractors and safety concerns directly to hospital boards and a stronger health care commission. "

"We will open up opportunities to see a GP near your place of work as well as your home, expand walk in centres, medical services at pharmacies and ensure a better service from NHS Direct"

They sound to me like the basis for an inspiring manifesto. If Gordon goes to the palace next week, we're ready to take it to the British people !

Tuesday, 15 January 2008
Any more skeletons ? Can we PLEASE get them out ?

I got involved in politics because I wanted to change things. I wanted to make Britain a fairer place, where poverty was a thing of the past and we had top quality public services. Which is why, yet again, I am sick to the back teeth of stories about party funding dominating the headlines. Who received what from whom? Who declared it to whom?... and, best of all, is there any more juicy stuff to come ? (yes, as it turned out with the undeclared donations to Tory George Osborne dwarfing Hain's £103,000...) [3]

David Abrahams' donations (the ones he gave through intermediaries to stay anonymous) were damaging to Labour , but forgivable, as the fault lies mainly with internal party officials- the main culprit being Peter Watt, the General Secretary and registered treasurer for the purposes of the Electoral Commission. Quite rightly, he was clearing his desk as soon as the story broke. However, the latest round of stories about £103,000 to Peter Hain's failed deputy leadership campaign is less so- Hain is a Cabinet Minister, and should know the rules.

Two things strike me about this story. First is that both are, in one sense, pretty trivial. None of the money is actually "dirty money" of any kind. The donations to Hain were legitimate, and the Abrahams money was from a man who (unlike Tory super-donor Lord Ashcroft) lives and pays tax in the UK. Had these donations been properly declared, they would not have made a footnote in the newspapers. Whether by deliberate rule-bending or simple sloppy accounting, all three cases have been turned from a non story into a "sleaze" story.

More irritating- £103,000 (plus!) for the Deputy Leadership campaign- the one that Hain finished FIFTH in ??? This was at a time when there was a significant possibility that we would be fighting an imminent general election- were there not better things that money could be donated to- like hard pressed constituency parties who will do the face-to-face and doorstep campaigning ? I haven't been able to find the official figures for all candidates (any offers?) but I know that Jon Cruddas outspent even Hain. In all there must have been in the region of half a million quid spent on the contest- a bit steep for a purely internal affair when there are other campaigning priorities.

Of course, this isn't just a Labour story- George Osborne, the Tories' wonder-boy shadow chancellor has had his knuckles rapped for failing to declare a whopping £487,000 in the Register of Members Interests, claiming he didn't realise it counted as a donation -even though it was personally earmarked to run his office!

I'm relieved to see a Tory getting sucked into this issue. However, though that bit is entertaining, it adds weight to the negative "they're all as bad as each other" opinion of elected politicians that contributes so much cynicism about our democracy, and leads to the record low turnouts of recent years.

A plea then- any MP, any Party…if you have anything to declare, can we please get it over in one go, and then we can get on with debating the more important questions facing Britain….

Thursday, 20 March 2008
In defence of the boy Ed...

They all seem to have the knives out for poor old Ed Balls. The Education Secretary- sorry- Secretary of State for Children Schools and Families (affectionately known as the Department for Curtains and Soft Furnishings in my line of work...) was alleged to have shouted "So What ?" to claims by "Dave" Cameron's predictable claim that British people are paying too much tax (schools, hospitals, support for pensioners etc. can all be funded with magic beans in the Tory world, of course...) For the record, Ed claims he actually shouted "So Weak" referring to the strength of Cameron's argument, and this is backed up by that bastion of propriety, the *Hansard* record of Parliamentary Debates.

Keith Newberry, the right-wing columnist in the Eastbourne Gazette could barely contain his joy- especially as the minister in question has a surname that allows him to wheel out that mature and intelligent skill of creating sexual innuendo from somebody's name- what an excellent school playground bully he must have made....[4]

Ian Lucas, my Tory friend pitches into the what-did-Ed-say debate on his I Love Eastbourne blog. In case you missed the story, telling us:

"guess what Ed Balls shouted out... He said 'So What?' I'm serious he really said, flippantly 'So what?' when Cameron was talking about people being taxed right up to the hilt" [5]

Ian, for all his Parliamentary ambitions, has not seemingly got the attachment to Hansard's accuracy that Mr Speaker would like...

Fair enough- as a senior cabinet member, Ed Balls is fair game for criticism. But I can't help feeling that, across the board, there's a bit of jealousy here.

Ed Balls, described by Ian Lucas as 'the most overrated MP in the House of Commons" is, in my opinion, one of the most intelligent members of the House, with a distinguished record as an economist. Balls not only won a highly competitive place to read PPE at Oxford, but followed that with a Kennedy Scholarship to Harvard. At 23 he was writing leader articles for the Financial Times, and shortly after started advising Gordon Brown on economic policy. While he may not always lack the common touch - "post neoclassical endogenous growth theory" not necessarily the best phrase to give Gordon for his speech- given that he was being employed at the time as an economics expert, I am heartened that he had the formidable intellect to understand the relevance and implications of post neoclassical endogenous growth theory, and it's a shame that he wasn't paired with a PR person to point out that we lesser mortals are not as conversant with post neoclassical endogenous growth theory (I just like typing it, actually) , and maybe it shouldn't have made the final text.

I feel that I should defend Ed this week, not least because, although he is a comrade of mine, I am often in friendly disagreement (despair) over elements of education policy, and as I'm off to Manchester for NUT conference, I've got this spooky feeling that I'm going to disagree with him a whole lot more over the next few days.

But, disagreements over academies, class size, broad-and-balanced curricula etc. aside, I am big enough to recognise Ed Balls for what he is- a man of formidable intellect. In the face of petty personal criticism, he should remember the old saying:

They shoot eagles, not sparrows.

Saturday 4 May 2008
Goodbye, Ken

May 3rd was a particularly painful day for me, with the London Mayoral result. Not just because the city of my birth and first few years was Tory- it had a Tory GLC when I was born- but because it saw the defeat of one of my top political heroes

"Red" Ken Livingstone will be remembered as one of the most colourful and charismatic Labour politicians of the last 30 years, and as one of the all-time most influential local government figures (up there with Herbert Morrison in London and Jack and Bessie Braddock in Liverpool)

Ken's early career is often derided by Labour so-called modernisers, and it is true that the politics of the GLC in the '80 was firmly on the Left of the Labour Party. But it combined a populist campaigning style (fireworks, festivals, and that fantastic banner on County Hall pointing out to Thatcher how many unemployed there were in London) with a raft of policies that, while daubed as "loony left" were actually ahead of their time:-

- Free bus travel for pensioners- it took another 20 years and a Labour government for this to be rolled out nationwide.
- Subsidised fares on the bus and tube to allow more people access to public transport. This was challenged in the courts by Tory councils like Bromley, who objected to the idea that ratepayers should have to support people who couldn't afford cars.
- Challenging racism, sexism and discrimination. "Political Correctness" to opponents, "common decency" to supporters- but how many comedians on mainstream TV tell "Pakistani" or "wife beating" jokes now ?
- Support for lesbian and gay rights. This was amongst the most controversial policies of the time: Tory bigotry and hatred was whipped up to the point where a Tory MP praised the firebombing of Gay News' offices, and the bullies' charter Section 28 was dreamed up.

Equally controversial was Livingstone's insistence that peace in Northern Ireland would only come through dialogue with Sinn Fein.[6] Ken and his allies were crucified in the press for arranging talks with Gerry Adams- at a time when, we now know, the Thatcher government had its own secret channels. Sinn Fein now provides Ian Paisley's Deputy First Minister in the Northern Ireland Assembly.

It was a tragedy when the Blair machine mobilised to stop Ken being Labour's first candidate for London Mayor. I spent most of 1999 wearing my "Let Ken Stand" badge, and attended the mass rally at Methodist Central Hall, where the campaign was supported by Jo Brand, Beryl Bainbridge, Dianne Abbott and Peter Tatchell (how times have changed !). Labour Party members overwhelmingly backed Ken, as did all the trade unions that balloted their members (the Fire Brigade Union gave him 94%) However, thanks to the previously vetted Assembly candidates votes, and the block vote of the AEEU and local Co-Op (neither of which chose to ballot members) Ken was pipped by Frank Dobson, who went on to just scrape third place in the election, only narrowly beating the Lib Dem.

Ken won as an independent, and, to his credit, Tony Blair admitted that he was wrong, and Ken rejoined Labour and was re-elected for a second term as a Labour Mayor.

The Tories were not going to shift Ken on policy. So, instead we saw a spin operation that would make Mandleson and Alistair Campbell look like amateurs. The smear campaign against Ken looked for, and found, everything but the kitchen sink to throw at his reputation:

- Ken was "anti-Semitic" (for comments he made to a reporter from the Evening Standard- part of a newspaper group that openly supported fascism in the 1930's, and is still well to the right of even the Tory mainstream)
- Ken was an "appeaser of radical Islam" (for sharing a platform with Egyptian Muslim cleric Yusuf al-Qaradawi, despite the praise they'd heaped on Ken for his leadership in the wake of the 7/7 atrocities. How quickly they forget...)
- Ken was "homophobic" (what?!?! Well, yes, apparently, because of al-Qaradawi, who, while denouncing terrorism has got a shocking record on gays and women)
- Ken appointed "cronies" (people he was politically close to: obviously completely different to MPs at Westminster who only employ political strangers who they don't know, don't like, don't agree with, and definitely aren't their wives and children...)
- Ken has illegitimate children (the words "stones" and "glass houses" come to mind when the Tories start pushing that one...)
- Ken has whisky in his glass during Mayoral Question Time.... (oh go on then, you can have that one. "Big wow" as we used to say when I was at school)

The hard-Right Evening Standard managed to bombard the people of London with anti-Ken stories with a ferocity not seen since the GLC days. Chief Ken-basher was disgraced ex-BBC journalist Andrew Gilligan, he of the dodgy dossier fame. No axe to grind with the Labour establishment then...

Alongside, was the hatchet job by Martin Bright in state owned broadcaster Channel 4's Dispatches programme. Bright's day job is as political editor of the New Statesman- left of centre magazine owned by Geoffrey Robinson MP (Lab) and read mainly by Labour supporters. How pleased his regular readers must be.

London will come to regret the ditching of Ken in place of the prat Boris (I could do a column on Boris, I rather suspect that I'd need a book) Ken can, however, console himself that the result in London was considerably better than in the other local elections (Labour actually gained a seat from the Tories in the London Assembly)

Meanwhile, Gordon Brown needs to take note: get the policy right, and don't expect any favours or fairness from the press. Ask Neil Kinnock about 1992, and don't let the media do the same to you...

Saturday 4 May 2008
WIPEOUT ???

Not a good night for Labour.

Four years ago, we had a bad night and lost a lot of good, hard-working Labour councillors. On May 1st, we lost some of those who survived last time.

Two lessons to be learnt:

The electorate is not silly. We made a huge mistake over the 10p tax issue, voters are worried that the economy is on the slide, and we have alienated hundreds of thousands of public sector workers (like me) who are usually the bedrock of the Labour vote. During the ascendancy of the New Labour project, we were not allowed to talk about the core vote. The Mandleson types would sneer that "they have nowhere else to go." Well now we know that they do: staying at home. With "Call-me-Dave" Cameron vying for the middle ground some Labour supporters are no longer as fearful of the prospect of a Tory government.

We need to re-engage with voters at the most local, street-by-street level. In particular, rather than playing the "more right wing than thou" game to try and attract Tory defectors, what about going after the centrist Labour voters that have moved to the Lib Dems in both inner city areas and middle England. After May 1st's results, in Liverpool, the Lib Dems needed a spineless defector to keep them in power, while in Hastings Paul Barlow took a seat off the Lib Dems and very nearly pulled an overall majority. How did he do this against the grain ? By working his backside off, door-to-door.

Eastbourne elects again on May 1st 2009. There are important European elections in June of that year, and the option of a General Election any time between now and May 2010. Time to stop despairing and start working !

Sunday, 25 May 2008
The bye-bye election ?

After the disastrous local elections of May 1st, Gordon Brown said that he would "listen and lead." When I heard this on the radio the first time, I misheard the second word... and wonder if what I heard would have been preferable.

Under the "Competence Procedure" used by my employer, and mirrored in many public sector employers, if a worker has demonstrated serious inability or weakness in an area of their job, then they jump straight to "Stage 3" of the procedure and are given an intensive 4 week period to bring about improvement. This is only used as a last resort- when the situation is far too serious for the normal improvement of performance measures to be put in place. If they fail, then dismissal (or demotion) procedures will follow.

The May 1st elections should have been seen by Gordon Brown as his own "Stage 3" trigger. Even more so, as the by-election had been moved with what some, rightly saw as indecent haste (as it was called even before Gwynneth Dunwoody's funeral!) there was now a natural "review of performance date" in the diary before the results of May 1st were known.

The local elections were a disaster, but not necessarily endgame for the Brown premiership. There were pockets of hope to build on in some areas- not least those councils where we were fighting the Liberal Democrats: Liverpool, Hastings etc, and the strong Labour performance in the inner-city wards of London. The May elections were an opportunity for, as GB himself acknowledged, some urgent listening to the electorate.

But the Crewe result was always going to be high stakes. The Tories had not taken a seat in a by election since 1978 in Ilford. They had even lost a safe Tory seat to the Lib Dems in Romsey in 2000, and nearly lost ultra-safe Bromley to them in 2006. As an unpopular government, we were always going to be up against it, but Crewe (despite being an island of socialism in true-blue Tory Cheshire) was considered a fairly safe seat- just outside Labour's strongest 100. Standing the daughter of the popular late local MP was the closest we would get to keeping the purely personal vote, and, despite the faux-outrage of a few ultra-New Labourites, it was right that the moneyed and privileged background of the millionaire Tory (local in as much as he has a £1.5m mansion 15 miles away) was mentioned. Probably in a more analytical and grown up way than the men in toff suits, however...

We were likely to lose Crewe. An 18% swing (that's the sort of swing that gave us "safe" Tory seats like Hastings in 1997, please note) cannot be put down to mid-term blues.

I would suggest:

- Say SORRY for the 10p tax band fiasco, and make a bigger deal of the changes that have been put in place to offset this. Either a significant and permanent increase in personal allowances, or bite the bullet and put the 10p rate back.
- Get tough on knife crime and the causes of knife crime. A background where more than a dozen teenagers have been stabbed to death on London's streets alone this year does not make people feel safe and secure. If you need proof that significant numbers of our teenagers are socially excluded, there are 14 pointlessly destroyed futures to evidence it.
- Tackle the housing crisis, by doing what is needed most, and building houses. We have acknowledged the need for more social housing since well before the 1997 election, but have only nibbled at the problem. I would wager that, amongst the new (reluctant) BNP voters at the last election, the perception that "immigrants can get a house and we can't" was the biggest single gripe (and, of course, untrue: nobody can get housed at the moment, that's the problem !)
- Employ a bit of foresight to avoid the increasing number of times when ministers find themselves "with a gaping hole in the foot, a smoking gun in their hand, and whine that they didn't realise it was loaded*". This applies not just in terms of national policy, but (in fact ten times more) to local issues such as unpopular hospital cuts, or the pointless and damaging privatisation of schools into Academies (often to be run by dodgy businessmen, tax exiles and those on the fringe of the evangelical movement !)

(*with thanks to Denis Healey)

So is Gordon doomed? It may not be personal: after all, last Autumn, he commanded 44% in the polls (had he called that snap election, on that basis we would have gained seats back from the Tories.) Equally, however, the people do not seem to be inspired by Gordon: the comparison with Blair in the mid-1990's is very unfair, but still pertinent. Can Gordon start to excite people ?

Regardless of whether the re-invention of "New Gordon" is possible, he needs to reverse the policy of the Blair years that avoided letting any other minister develop too positive a public image, lest they challenged the inevitability of Gordon's heir-apparent status. When Wilson resigned in 1976, the resulting contest saw 6 challengers, (Callaghan, Foot, Healey, Benn, Jenkins and Crossland) all of whom were household names, and were, to varying extents, serious contenders. When Gordon ascended, the nearest challenges came from a 67-year old minister from the Callaghan government Michael Meacher) , and the cheerleader of the hard-left, who many non-Party members outside of Hayes and Harlington had never heard of before (John McDonnell). Good for Gordon, but says something about the state of the Party. We need a team of hard-hitting, recognisable ministers, with a synergy that can blow the Tories right out of the water.

The people of Eastbourne could teach Gordon Brown a thing or two about by-elections.

In 1990, our Tory MP Ian Gow was murdered by the IRA. The Lib Dems took Eastbourne with an even bigger swing. Less than two years later, the Tories had the seat back, and were in Government having won a record 4th term.

The cautionary note is that, barely a month after what had seemed the Tories' point-of-no-return at Eastbourne, Margaret Thatcher was gone. Can Gordon lead us into the same sort of turnaround of fortune, or is there a Heseltine waiting in the Labour Party wings ?

Sunday, 29 June 2008
Waiting at the Church ?

In 1978, Jim Callaghan, ahead in the polls was expected to call a general election. He teased supportive trade unionists in his speech to that Autumn's TUC, by singing the Lily Langtree music hall song "Waiting at the Church". Everybody applauded, as they didn't get what he was saying.

There was no election in 1978- and the winter that followed saw a wave of mainly, but not exclusively, public sector strikes that became dubbed "The Winter of Discontent" by a **hysterical tabloid press**. There was the famous photo of the rubbish piled in Trafalgar Square (complete with a **stuffed rat placed there by the photographer**- before the days of photoshop, and a few days of action by council gravediggers, that postponed a few funerals- the rest is history...) The following year, Callaghan lost a vote of confidence in Parliament, and "that woman" became Prime Minister.

Experts generally concur that **Sunny Jim could have won it in 1978**, and he let the last chance slip through his fingers.

When I put up for the Eastbourne Labour nomination, I kept my diary mentally clear for a November 2007 election. In the autumn of that year, we were riding at 47% in the polls: had that been repeated in a General Election we would not only have increased our majority, but **we would have won seats that we didn't even take in 1997**.

Now, less than 1 in 4 voters are planning to vote for us.

The Henley by-election was unlikely to be a good day for us. But things are far worse than predicted- and make Crewe and Nantwich look like a Labour landslide.

We have, occasionally, lost our deposit (by polling less than 5% in an election.) We did it in Eastbourne in 1992, when people had a tactical-vote stab at keeping by-election victor **David** *"whoops-there-goes-my-football-club"* **Bellotti** in Parliament. Funnily enough, we **kept** our deposit in the 1990 by-election that said "bye bye" to Maggie.

- We lose our deposit in rock solid Tory seats that the Lib Dems win on a tactical swing (eg Newbury) We don't do it when the Lib Dems are also beaten out of sight.

- We don't come behind the Greens. We have never been beaten by the Green Party in a Parliamentary contest until now. With them champing at our heels in Brighton Pavilion, (not too close to our heels- they were still third at the last General election behind us and the Tories) this is not a good sign.
- We don't come behind the BNP. While we have lost council seats to the fascists, we have always kept our critical mass in Parliamentary sized contests. To do this in an area where there aren't BNP councillors or obvious flashpoints is a deeply sinister development. The BNP have never stood in Eastbourne, for instance (although the National Front did in the past) Are we likely to see them trying their luck here ?

At the risk of sounding like a broken record- we need to do something. The RAF used to parody Rudyard Kipling's poem "If":

If you can keep your head, when all about you are losing theirs… you haven't grasped the seriousness of the situation.

Is this why Gordon, Harriet, Ed and friends seem so **calm** ? Anyway- to cheer me up, let's head back to the 70's…

One interesting fact about Thatcher's sweep to power in 1979 (it was a comfy majority, but certainly no landslide) was that throughout the election, and until he resigned as Labour leader in 1980, **Jim Callaghan was comfortably ahead in the personality polls**. A significant majority of voters backed him personally over Thatcher. However, despite their misgivings about the Lady from Grantham, her policies on home ownership, trade union reform and the economy were enough to swing it.

Conversely, in 2008 Gordon Brown is not going to be placed in any Most Charismatic Politician competitions. Unlike his predecessor, he is not a darling of the media, and is never likely to be. What Gordon has is the reputation for having a brain the size of Glasgow, and a wobbly- but not yet discredited- reputation as a safe pair of hands.

Bill Clinton was elected in 1992 on a slogan that went "It's the Economy, Stupid…" If Brown can come up with a strategy that avoids the R- thing that we aren't allowed to mention, can help us ride out the "Credit Crunch" and avoid a meltdown in the housing market, he may still be able to use that moniker a little longer. *(Did you notice how I got away with that last phrase just moments after mentioning Clinton… although I think I got away with it..)*

So to the policy question. Labour cyber-hero Luke Akehurst finds himself agreeing with **Diane Abbott** on this. No problem for me- as I often agree with her. Diane told Hackney North Labour Party[7]:

- We'd be nuts to change leader again so quickly
- We all need to stop panicking and that will be helped by MPs going on recess and not all being in London stirring each other up
- Gordon should focus on using the next two years to deliver two or three landmark policies that are the things he really wants to achieve in politics and will be "recognisably Labour, not necessarily left wing, but inspiring and heartening to Labour people"

Good advice. Will it be heeded in time ?

Saturday, 26 July 2008
Brown's Eastbourne

...is the title that a number of bloggers (mainly conservative) are giving to the **Glasgow East** result.

I was chatting to a Lib Dem friend on Thursday morning, in which I assured her that we were **not going to lose Glasgow East**. It would be a reduction of a huge Labour majority, and would give us a realistic "line in the sand" about how much trouble we are in, but the polls and the fact that we were up against the SNP who were the alternative "government party" in Scotland meant that an actual loss was not on the cards.

Ooops. Big, big bags of oops.

A tiny majority for the SNP- this is true. The fact that either of the Left candidates' votes (SSP or Solidarity) could have swung it for us another straw to clutch at *(actually, given the latest story about a leadership plot, maybe I shouldn't use that metaphor)*

As it is so nice to see **Eastbourne** in the national political news twice in a week (see also Boris Johnson slagging off all of Britian's seaside resorts- really helpful in promoting local economies, thanks Boris...) it's worth looking at the Eastbourne comparison.

The 1990 Eastbourne by-election (mentioned elsewhere in this blog, so no full history lesson: if you want the facts and figures go to Wikipedia) was widely credited as a significant event in **bringing down Thatcher**. A safe Tory seat (although not impenetrable: the opposition tended to be quite split- not least in 1979 when the late **Len Caine** nearly equalled the Liberal vote) fell to the Lib Dems in a shock result. Whether the poll tax, the malaise with a Thatcher administration that had just gone on too long, whether the fact that the local Labour candidate was unilaterally deposed by Labour HQ- killing off any serious local Labour campaign, it didn't matter. **Thatcher had lost a blue-rinse safe seat, and had to go.**

Eastbourne was Orange. Eastbourne was a non-Tory zone. Eastbourne was under new management. Eastbourne now had a new MP: **David "whoops-there-goes-my-football-club" Bellotti.**

The Tories went on to lose anything going in a by election. **Ribble Valley**, **Vale of Glamorgan**, **Monmouth, Langbaurgh, Mid Staffordshire**: indeed, post 1992 it continued Wirral West, Littleborough and Saddleworth, Christchurch, Newbury. **The Tories failed to hold a by-election seat from 1989** *(when William Hague was elected to parliament- and only then because David Owen's SDP stood against the newly formed Liberal Democrats)* **right up until Uxbridge in 1997.**

So where is the hope ? Well, I recall the words of the defeated Eastbourne Tory candidate Richard Hickmet on the radio the morning after his defeat morning. *(Although I was not quite 13, I was already a political junkie.)*

"Enjoy your six to 18 months in Parliament, Mr Bellottii"

He was right. For, in 1992, Nigel Waterson recaptured Eastbourne, defeating the sitting MP with an overall majority. That same night **all of the other by-election losses returned to the Tories**, as John Major was swept back to power- although his commons majority was well down, the Tories received a **higher number of votes** than any party before them. Higher than Thatcher in 1983 or Attlee in 1945 *(Ironically, the record was previously held by Labour in 1951- an election they lost to the Tories: welcome to the wonderful world of first past the post constituency elections.)*

False hope ? Mindless optimism ? Maybe. But the message to Gordon (and the plotters ?) has to be that a by-election low point **does not mean that the game is up.** It does mean that the political finger has to be pulled out- that something drastic and effective needs to be done. And it needs to be done now.

Monday 15 September 2008
Night of the blunt knives

At the time of writing, 12 Labour MPs have joined the mini-campaign to force a leadership challenge to Gordon Brown.[8]

Aside from **Graham Stringer**, Manchester MP who has been seemingly calling for a challenge to Gordon since the day after his election as leader, the faces crawling out of the woodwork have been interesting.

Siobhan McDonough, uber-Blairite, whose sister was the General Secretary of the Labour Party in Blairier days. **Joan Ryan**, a little-known loyalist, **Fiona McTaggart**, another prominent Blairite. Joining them is serial rebel (and long term critic of Brown, in a wound that hasn't been lanced since his brief spell as Social Security Minister) **Frank Field**.

John McDonnell of the hard-Left campaign group, has thrown his two pennyworth in (at least he can claim to be **consistent**- he's always opposed Brown.) Interestingly, only **Gordon Prentice** from those who nominated McDonnell for the leadership has come out for a contest: according to Luke Akehurst, veteran Left winger **Diane Abbott** is fiercely against a contest, as is serial rebel **Bob Marshall-Andrews**, who earlier called for David Milliband to be sacked for his article that allegedly set out his stall for a leadership push.

What's going on ? Well, on Radio 4 yesterday, Joan Ryan was claiming that all that is going on is that MPs are requesting that nomination papers are sent out to all Labour MPs, as provided for annually in the rules.

What a load of rubbish. The convention has been that this does NOT happen when a Labour leader is also the Prime Minister. **It never happened during Blair's tenure**. It's not even as simple as nominating an alternative candidate (there isn't one) or proving that you have 70 MPs to nominate them (there aren't)

Labour's annual conference must then vote on whether to proceed with a leadership conference. The votes at conference are shared between affiliated unions and societies, (none of which I am aware has indicated any interest in a leadership challenge,) and the delegates from the **constituency parties** on the ground, many of whom saw local meltdown in the council elections in the spring, but, in the main recognise that an **orgy of self-indulgent infighting** will do little to restore the electorate's faith in the Labour Party.

I'd love to see a change in policy direction for the government. I'd like to see Gordon unveil a raft of radical and imaginative policies that get our supporters excited and enthused once again. We're not going to get that by **diverting all attention away from politics** and on to petty scores and ambitions from a bunch of has-beens and never-weres.

The leadership plotters (makes them sound far more grand than they are) are as far from proposing a **quick and sharp solution** to the direction of the Labour Party as is possible, as they has no chance of forcing a contest under the rules they claim to be following. What it is engineered to do is ferment discontent and doubt, and to **undermine** the leadership of Gordon Brown to the point where he is forced to resign. Not so much quick and sharp, as a lingering death. **Cowardly**, too, as they haven't got the guts to just admit that they want to damage their leader beyond rescue, and hang the consequences. **They aren't the sort of people I enjoy sharing a Party with.**

On Sunday 21st September, following comments made on the site, I added:
Glad to see I have provoked two welcome comments on the last article.

John McDonnell MP points out that he is being falsely counted among the rebels, probably by lazy journalists who make assumptions because of his previous near-candidacy against Brown for the leadership. Many people on the left have been agitating for John to throw his hat into the ring **when there is a contest**, but I accept that in no way is this the same as him calling for one at this point.

My friend **Daniel Blaney** makes an intelligent, compelling and sometimes earthy contribution, with which I have some sympathy, but **not necessarily agreement**. I regret that the rules of the Labour Party (however you interpret them) make it **difficult, if not impossible**, for a sitting leader to be challenged. I don't like being in a party which, in that respect, appears to hold its leaders less accountable than the Tory Party. The question on whether the (conflicting) rules require nomination papers to go out every year we are in Government is **not clear cut-** mainly because those rules didn't exist last time we had a Labour government.

Daniel and I part company in that **I don't believe Gordon Brown qualifies, in any way, as "hopeless"**, and I'd rather have Brown's (slightly bigger) big tent than a full-speed-ahead lurch to the right under one of the unreconstructed Blairites any day.

Monday, 29 September 2008
No time for a Novice

It is rare that I find myself in agreement with local Tories, but as former Tory leader **Ian Lucas** has set himself up as a Gordon Brown cheerleader, I will happily reprint his words.

In his online column for the *Eastbourne Herald*, Ian comments:

"It's probably best to leave Gordon Brown where he is, after all he has as much chance of steering the UK through these bad economic times than any other Labour MP. And that's much more important than the internal strife of the Labour Party." [9]

In fairness to Ian, I rather suspect that he intended the reader to place a rather stronger emphasis on the word Labour at the end of the first sentence than I did, but the sentiment remains. He is rather cruel about the prospects of any of the touted *heirs apparent* in the same article, but I won't repeat them here- click over and read his whole column if you want to know Ian's opinion of **David Milliband**.

I enjoyed Gordon Brown's speech, and that is never taken for granted. He is not the orator that his predecessor was, nor indeed does he have the set-'em-alight skill that John Prescott had with a mass meeting (and I challenge the journalists who mocked his grammar to go to a live, tub thumping Prescott address and not be inspired.)

Nor, indeed, does Brown go for the political stunt- which is why the intro from his low-profile wife Sarah was a surprise. In fact, this move **chimed rather well** with the conference, who, in contrast to Mrs Blair do not feel that they see too much of Mrs Brown, rather that they don't know her that well, are genuinely interested in finding out more.

The one line that sticks out in a speech that had a good spread of policy announcements (that were, inevitably, overlooked in much of the reporting) was the comment about **"No time for a Novice"**

Whatever faults Gordon Brown may have, he can still draw a lot of political capital from his time as Chancellor, when the general public opinion was that he was a hugely **intelligent and capable** man. Gordon Brown knows about economics: indeed he has been Labour's chief economic brain since 1992, when he took over the brief from the **best Prime Minister we never had**:

the late, great John Smith. Brown has been around a long time, and has unrivalled experience, having entered Parliament in 1983. **Some of the names being touted for the leadership weren't even in Parliament in 1997** ! (nor, indeed was David Cameron)

No doubt there will continue to be rumour and speculation from what Prescott memorably termed "the Bitterites". But perhaps, at a time when the economy is political issue #1 and we have an experienced economist in number 10, they will take their plotting somewhere else, and let Gordon get on with the job

Sunday 21 October 2007
Too much recycling ?

An interesting pre-budget statement from Alistair Darling- marred a bit by accusations that he'd recycled (nicked ?) some of the Tories' conference policies. Indeed, the inheritance tax and non-domiciled tax were strikingly similar to the Tory proposals. But, on IHT, the figure of £600,000 is much more reasonable and in line with our philosophy than the typical unreconstructed Tory proposal not to take a penny off the sons and daughters of (near) millionaires.

Inheritance Tax is a difficult one. The levels used to be set roughly to ensure that people could leave the family home to their children- and £300,000 used to more than cover most ordinary working people's homes and cash. However, the housing boom- (partly due to the reluctance of the government to really take on the vested interests that oppose every social-housing project) did indeed mean that more and more middle-class families were finding that their homes were going to beat the threshold, so Darling's increase is indeed appropriate.

But the Tory million ? Yes, the cash and assets earned in one's lifetime are taxed at source, and it is natural that parents want to leave their hard earned wealth to their children. But turn this around- their children may inherit thousands of pounds that they have not worked a day for. If they had gone out, learned a trade, entered a profession or started a business and earned those sums, they would have paid 40% tax on much of it. In a climate where no party is prepared (rightly) to talk about reducing public spending, is it fairer to tax unearned wealth, or give it tax breaks, while continuing to tax hard-earned income? I think that we've probably got the balance right.

Also in the statement-
Non-domiciled tax of £30,000: £5,000 more than the Tories. I still don't like it, though, as I'd rather the overseas oligarch paid tax on the same basis as the guy who cleans his toilets… Green levy on airline flights (previously a Tory policy, previously a Lib Dem policy, previously a Green Party policy- some call that poaching, I'd call it consensus. And it annoys that weaselly bloke who runs Ryan Air…) Modest benefit increases- pension credit up, child benefit doubled. Extra £200million to support continuing free bus travel for pensioners, (although not yet to expand Ken Livingstone's initiative in London for free travel for under 16's- which is disappointing)

THE OPPOSITION

Why did I join Labour? The history and values, of course- equality, fairness, the role of Government as a means to make ordinary people's lives better. Against that- the alternative of the Tories. I grew up with a Conservative government, and the "me first" attitudes of the Thatcher government (combined with the indignity of working in low paid jobs before the Minimum Wage,) helped me focus on what the alternative to Labour was- and it wasn't pretty. These columns help remind me why I want to keep a Labour government!

Wednesday 20 June 2007
Why I still support PR

With the reports about Gordon Brown apparently inviting Paddy Ashdown into his cabinet, there has been some speculation about whether the instinctive (and correct) opposition to this from grassroots Labour supporters is a nail in the coffin for debate about proportional representation. I firmly believe that it isn't.

Ashdown should not be invited into the cabinet, because under the current system, we elected a majority Labour government, and it should serve as a Labour government. If we had elections under a PR system, then people would know that they were likely to see a result that would require co-operation between parties, and there would have been a vigorous debate about the possibilities during the campaign. No such debate has happened here.

I have always supported a proportional element for local government elections. In many parts of the country, majority rule by one party is a rare occurrence- and the better for it. The main parties have serve alongside minor parties, independents, residents associations etc, reflecting the political and community interests of the whole area. This model works well for local government, and an element of proportionality (not getting rid of the ward system completely, which is important for local people to have genuine local representation) would allow parties with significant but spread votes in a town to have a voice (like Labour and the Greens in Eastbourne.)

At Westminster, there are more compelling arguments for First Past The Post, but having endured 4 general elections where the local Lib Dem argument has basically been "A Labour vote is a wasted vote: vote for us as we can beat the Tories" has served to stifle and strangle genuine political debate, and has left a significant proportion of the electorate feeling disenfranchised. A PR system with safeguards to smaller parties having a stranglehold on power, still strikes me as preferable in a modern democracy.

The Lib Dems have always supported PR, although, were it to happen, it may well be their undoing. In Eastbourne, a significant part of their vote is "tactical" Labour voters. In the inner city seats, it is tactical Tories. Many people who would vote Green or for other minor parties often end up voting Lib Dem in the General Election as a protest vote against the majority local party.

Add to this the haemorrhaging of Lib Dem support that will come from one side of this balance as soon as a hung Parliament (distinctly possible even under the current system- currently the bookies favourite outcome for 2009) means that they have to jump one way or the other. Join a Labour coalition, and kiss goodbye to the soft-Tory votes in the inner cities. Join with the Tories, and they will never be able to include those "Labour Can't Win Here" graphs in their *Focus* leaflets, and CON HOLD Eastbourne for ever.

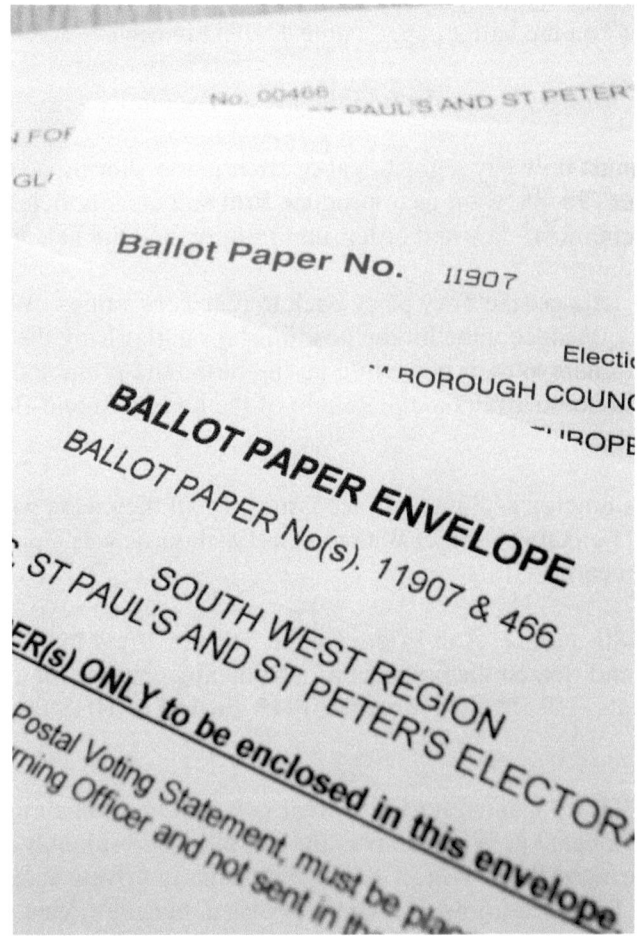

Sunday, 22 July 2007
Nasty Party sharpens knives

"Dave" Cameron is under pressure from traditional Tories to end his attempts to move the Conservative Party to the elusive centre ground.

Certainly the two by-elections last week, where, despite a high profile campaign by the Tories in Ealing Southall (where they control the local council), the party that temporarily branded itself "David Cameron's Conservatives" on the ballot paper, came THIRD in both.

Right-winger Ann Widdecombe told the Press Association:

"[Cameron] must now pay a great deal of attention to shoring up our traditional vote. People want us to produce firm and clear policies on issues that worry them most - law and order, immigration and the health service" [2]

I quite agree- let's get the Tory party back to real Tory values. When she was a minister, Widdecombe hit the headlines for authorising the shackling of women prisoners to their bed while giving birth, and promoted a hard-right agenda in home affairs to the delight of the hang-'em-and-flog-'em Tory grassroots.

The Tories hammered asylum and race issues for all they were worth in the 1997 and 2001 elections- Nigel Waterson in Eastbourne was a particular fan of the Asylum card.

As for the health service, Ann Widdecombe was not afraid to think the unthinkable, and floated the prospect of introducing charges for a range of NHS treatments- effectively ending the 1945 ideal of an NHS free at the point of use.

Old Etonian "Dave" Cameron tries to wear new clothes (some might say rather Blairite ones) but Widdecombe and her allies (presumably including the unreconstructed Right-winger Nigel Waterson, in private at least) still speak for the Tory grassroots, and an unspecified, but significant group of MPs. Indeed, several "gutless" ones (according to a shadow cabinet member,) have apparently written to the Chairman of the 1922 committee (a sort of trade union for backbench Tories- but don't let them hear you call it that!) demanding a vote on Cameron's future as leader.

Yep- the knives are out, as is routine when the Tories have their backs to the wall. Here's hoping for a swift end to the Cameron project, then voters will be given a clear choice, between a progressive Labour government under Gordon Brown, and the real Tories- as described by former Conservative Party Chairman Theresa May- "The Nasty Party."

Friday, 17 August 2007
Same Old Redwood

Perhaps because of renewed speculation that Gordon Brown will call an early election, the Tories have finally started to make policy proposals.

Heading up their economic policy review is John Redwood- of the Tories' unashamed hard-right wing. Redwood was briefly a cabinet minister in the last Tory government, but resigned so that he could challenge the then Prime Minister John Major for the Tory leadership, on a more right wing platform. (The last unsuccessful challenger to a sitting Tory leader had been Anthony Meyer, who ran against Thatcher and was promptly deselected by his local Tory association. The "new" Conservatives are evidently more forgiving.)

The main thrust of the "new" Tory policy is exactly the same as the old one that they lost the last three General Elections with: promising sweeping tax cuts- estimated as adding up to £21 billion. That is, of course, £21 billion less for schools, hospitals,, pensions etc. Nothing new from the Tory Party there, though.

The second strand is the promise of slashing regulations on business- including creating a minister for deregulation. "What a marvellous idea," I hear you cry… so what might this bonfire of regulations mean ? Perhaps their starting point would be getting rid of the regulations introduced SINCE the Tories were last in power in 1997, so:-

- **Repealing** the Social Chapter regulations- the Tories wanted an opt out- would end the right of working parents to take emergency unpaid leave when a child is ill.
- **Repealing** the Working Time directive- another bugbear of the Tories- would end the right to four weeks paid holiday that is currently enjoyed by every worker. Under the last Tory government, workers were not entitled to a SINGLE day's paid holiday.
- **Repealing** the right to trade union recognition by a ballot- which ensures that workers could choose to negotiate through a union if a clear majority wanted it.
- **Repealing** protection against inferior treatment of part-time workers- many of them women with family responsibilities.
- **Repealing** equality legislation- under the Tories it was perfectly legal to dismiss someone on the grounds of the sexual orientation.
- **Repealing** the requirement on firms over a certain size to offer workers access to a pension scheme- making sensible provision for our future, aging population.

And what about the minimum wage ? John Major called it immoral. Michael Howard claimed it would cause massive unemployment. Michael Heseltine thought that £2.50 an hour was more than adequate. John Redwood was fiercely opposed to minimum wage then- so has he, or any of his Tory colleagues really changed their mind ? There was no minimum wage AT ALL under the last Tory government.

The Tories claim in their report today that they would "strive to create fair conditions for workers." Looking at their past record, I'd have to reply: "That'd be a first…."

Saturday, 8 September 2007
CROOK

In January of this year, I started campaigning to make people aware of the dodgy politics of one of our elected Euro-MPs Mr Ashley Mote.

Mote was elected in June 2004 to the South East regional list of MEP's- as a member of the UKIP slate. In July (yep, a month later) he was expelled from UKIP after they found out that he was facing trial for benefit fraud.

Despite our elections to the European Parliament being based on a party list system, there is no way of removing an MEP if he subsequently leaves the Party of the platform upon which he was elected. Despite being in the European Parliament because people put a cross by UKIP, he was able, a month later, to continue "representing" you, me and others in our region as an independent.

Bad enough, you might think. But in January of this year, he went further, joining the new "Identity, Tradition and Sovereignty" group in the Parliament. This far-right grouping includes the French National Front (Jean Marie Le Pen and friends) the Austrian Freedom Party of Jorg Haider, and Italian Fascist icon Alessandra Mussolini (yes, daughter of the same...) Bulgarian, Romanian and Belgian far-right wingers make up the team. Our MEP is the vice-chairman.

The BNP have indicated that this is the group they would affiliate to, were (God forbid) they ever to succeed in getting an MEP elected from Britain. At the last elections, the BNP didn't come close to electing a member from any of the regions in Britain, including those where they have had some local government successes (the South East is not one of those regions.) Yet, we have, allegedly speaking for us, and being paid from our taxes, an MEP who the neo-fascist BNP have a great deal of respect for. While Mote claims not to have any links with the BNP, this does not stop him adding to the royalties on some of his books which are sold via the BNP website ![4]

This week, Ashley Mote was jailed for nine months for £65,503 of benefit fraud. As a man who campaigned about the cost of the European Union to the taxpayer clearly does not apply the same principles to himself. Yet- while Mote languishes in prison, he will KEEP his seat in the European Parliament. Even his former colleague from UKIP, Nigel Farage was "disgusted and horrified" at the leniency of his sentence. [5]

This despicable thief (yes- that's what he actually is- he stole sixty-five grand of your money) has no shame. His website carried the following statement:

"Owing to unforeseen circumstances there will be a short intermission in my trouble-making in the European Parliament on behalf of the constituents of South-East England." [6]

Surely we now need to look at the rules to ensure that the South East (and every other region) can be properly represented, without ever having its seats and money wasted on a dishonest, xenophobic, fascist-sympathising crook again.

Sunday, 16 September 2007
When Maggie met Gordy

Mary Turner, President of the GMB Union and a member of Labour's National Executive was scornful of Gordon Brown's praise of Margaret Thatcher as a "conviction politician". She told the TUC Conference that "she should have been convicted….and got 20 years."

In the Daily Mirror yesterday, columnist Fiona Millar was equally scathing of Thatcher's number 10 visit, hoping that it would be "her last under this government." [7]

Yep, there were a lot of strong feelings- especially when Brown's praise of the "Iron Lady" led to a personal visit on Thursday after which she emerged with a smiling Gordon, clutching a bouquet of flowers.

Margaret Thatcher stood politically for virtually everything I disagree with:-
- Economic policies that actively worked against the goal of full employment- leading to more than three million unemployed.
- Privatisation on the cheap- some necessary like BT, others like the water companies (still all monopoly providers) leading to poorer service and higher charges
- Tax cuts for the rich while rates of VAT and indirect taxes on ordinary people went up,
- Attacks on rights of people at work in tandem with anti-trade union laws to ensure that working people had little means to defend themselves,
- Hypocritical harking back to so-called Victorian values, manifesting themselves in inflammatory speeches that gave succour to racists and homophobes, and culminating in hateful legislation such as the "sus law" and Section 28
- The abolition of bodies that disagreed with her- such as the GLC and the metropolitan councils (and people who disagreed with her, like her first two chancellors- Nigel Lawson and Geoffrey Howe)
- Scuppering progress towards peace and the reduction of nuclear arsenals (Thatcher reportedly rushed off to intervene in talks between Reagan and Gorbachev when it looked like there might be deal on significant bilateral reductions in nuclear weapons.
- Destruction of major industries (steel, shipbuilding, motor vehicles, great swathes of the British manufacturing base, and of course the coalfields, the latter driven less by economics than by spite.)

However, when it comes to her little tea party with the PM this week, I have to confess to not sharing the nausea of some of my colleagues. In the United States, former presidents, whatever their party, maintain a high public status, and are routinely invited to great occasions of state. Tony Blair entertained Thatcher in Downing Street- a courtesy extended by the lady herself to predecessors Harold Wilson and Jim Callaghan (curiously though, it seems, not Ted Heath.) If Gordon was inviting Maggie along to get her detailed input on policy issues, then I would be worried. But it seems perfectly healthy for previous leaders to be received by the current incumbent, perhaps to share lessons from their own experiences on the domestic and world stage.

If nothing else- the Tories are rattled. Former Thatcher-era cabinet minister Sir Malcolm Rifkind opined that "only Maggie Smith's portrayal of the British ambassador's widow in Tea with Mussolini was as brazen as Maggie Thatcher's acceptance of tea with Gordon" [8]

The Daily Mirror, meanwhile, reported that the original plan for a low key visit, with Mrs Thatcher "smuggled in the back door," was replaced when Mrs Thatcher's office indicated that she would welcome the TV cameras. Having tried to airbrush her out of history, "Dave" Cameron is now apparently desperately pushing to get her to Tory Party conference to endorse him- an invitation that was conspicuously absent just days before.[9]

If tea and a chat at number 10 can get the Tories in the flap that the media suggest, then Gordon clearly knew what he was doing. I may even forgive him for the flowers…

Sunday 7 October 2007
Lib-Dems to join with Cameron?

My old colleague and running-mate from Hampden Park, Dave Salmon knows what the Liberal Democrats are like- he was one of Labour's last councillors in Langney in the late 1970's, when the Liberal tide began to engulf that part of Eastbourne. Dave, unlike me, is also an avid listener of Radio 4, so heard an interview that I missed- with the Lib Dem treasury spokesman, Vincent Cable.

Not a traditional Tory- Vince Cable was an advisor to former Labour leader John Smith when he served as a Cabinet Minister under Jim Callaghan. Since then, the boy Vince has defected to the Lib Dems via the SDP, and is now seen as one of the new breed (albeit a man of some mature years) of thrusting right-of-centre Lib Dem modernisers.

Dave's attention was caught by Cable refusing in any way to rule out the possibility of the Lib Dems going into some kind of coalition with "Dave" Cameron's Tories in the event of a hung parliament. Perhaps this is no surprise…..

In BIRMINGHAM, the Tories and Lib Dems run the City in a shaky coalition against Labour who have the most elected councillors.

In CAMDEN, formerly a solid Labour area, the Lib Dems are in coalition with the Tories, against a Labour opposition.

In LEEDS, they've gone one better- a coalition of Lib Dems, Tories and Greens, running the city in an anyone-but-Labour alliance.

… as well as in several other areas of the country. In much of the inner cities, the Lib Dems have replaced the Tories as the opposition to Labour, and openly cultivate the "tactical" votes of Conservative supporters.

Will Stephen Lloyd oust Nigel Waterson in Eastbourne, only to take up his own ministerial post in a Tory-led government? Dave Salmon tells me that he has written to Mr Lloyd, giving him the opportunity to rule this out, and I will happily publish his reply. I wonder if he dare…..?

Sunday 21 October 2007
Merciless for Ming

Vooom ! You didn't see that one coming…

The Lib Dems are at it again, knifing yet another leader. Last time it was Charles Kennedy, for liking a drink (which everybody knew,) this time it was Ming Campbell for being old (which everybody knew.)

Sir Menzies Campell was indeed an elder statesman of the Liberal movement. A distinguished lawyer, a former Olympic athlete, an experienced and respected Parliamentarian. I didn't care for his politics or his party, but he brought a gravitas to the leadership, which people seemed to quite like. In the post-Blair era, the days of leaders needing to be photogenic, thrusting young things who listen to the Arctic Monkeys, seemed to have been replaced by a more serious, dare I say grown up, politics.

Ming took on the critics of his age at his own Party conference and won. He seemed unassailable, yet, just a few weeks later his resignation was being announced on his behalf by Simon Hughes and the new acting leader Vince Cable (ex-Labour, ex-SDP, turned Lib Dem right winger) It was reminiscent of the "resignation" of Harry Perkins in A Very British Coup (Chris Mullin- read it if you haven't!) Ming was nowhere to be seen, although we were told that the resignation was entirely his own decision, and nobody had pushed him…

The Lib Dems seem to have something of a political death wish. Languishing dangerously close to the single-figures graveyard in the polls, and with a resurgent Tory party, conventional wisdom would suggest that the combined strategies of targeting disillusioned Labour supporters and promoting a leader who was politically bigger than the Blair-lite "Call-me-Dave" Cameron would be in order. Instead, it seems highly likely that they are ditching the instantly recognisable Ming with one of several nonentities (with fairly marginal seats.) All of the challengers being mooted seem to be from the Lib Dem's Right wing, which suits me fine, as economic liberalism is not likely to attract any disillusioned traditional Labourites.

Indeed, poised to lose a chunk of their MPs, with the combination of Tory resurgence and a wad of Lord Ashcroft's cash in key marginals, this could be endgame for what looked only a few years ago, as a Party that could have ended the two-Party system. Doesn't look like it now, does it?

Wednesday, 23 January 2008
Clegg lurches to the Right

As he's now been in the job a few weeks, I guess I ought to devote a little time to Nick "Genghis" Clegg, the new Lib Dem leader.

In Eastbourne, the Lib Dems have benefited in the past from many tactical-voting Labour supporters, under the impression that "nice Mr Lloyd" would be more left-wing than "nasty Mr Waterson." This is probably true, as I have met very few people who are not more left wing than Nigel Waterson. I haven't met Nick Clegg, but I rather think he could actually be one.

So- who is Nick Clegg? Well, after Westminster Public School and Cambridge, Nick Clegg worked within the European Union bureaucracy, and rose to working in former Tory cabinet minster Leon Brittain's private office as a policy adviser and speechwriter. Yup- his job entailed telling one of Maggie's "true believers" what to think, and how to say it….

Clegg also has some very dodgy right-wing ideas of his own. A contributor to the Orange Book- a Lib Dem hard-Right manifesto, Clegg has thrown his support behind destroying the NHS. He told The Independent:

"I think breaking up the NHS is exactly what you do need to do" later adding that the Lib Dems should "not rule out" scrapping the NHS and moving to an insurance model. [10]

He's very keen on the privatisation of the Post Office, (mind you, Ming liked that one…) and even before the leadership coup, he and his gang had engineered the end of the Lib Dems support for redistributive taxation (remember that 50p band for top earners that they've gone quiet on…..?)

If you're thinking it's unfair to judge him on what he said before being tempered by the responsibility of leadership- don't worry. "Genghis" set out his stall in one of his first major speeches of the year- telling us:

"the state must back off and allow the genius of grassroots innovation …. to take off in providing an array of top class schools and hospitals." [11]

Translation: "privatise schools, privatise hospitals, privatise anything else you can get your hands on, and if we call it innovation, maybe they won't notice!"

Clegg, however, does show outstanding loyalty to the political principle of....well... advancing the career of Nick Clegg, really. Even as a new boy in the 2005 parliament, he was quick to settle in and find the knife drawer- as one of the group of hard-right Lib Dems who knifed Charles Kennedy (Clegg was a signatory to the political death warrant that demanded Kennedy's resignation)

Clegg's loyalty switched smoothly to Ming Campbell, who appointed Genghis to the front bench- and was rewarded, according to Kevin Maguire, by this kind of loyalty:

"While waiting on Bournemouth station for the London train, it was impossible for your columnist not to overhear the Lib Dems' home affairs chap itemising, between sips of Red Bull, his leader Sir Ming Campbell's political crimes. Ming the Mediocre, according to Clegg, is hesitant and disorganised, commits avoidable errors and lacks momentum ...with friends like Clegg, who needs Simon Hughes?"

So which way will Clegg swing after the next election? Stephen Lloyd insists that it will not be into coalition with the Tories, and local Tory Ian Lucas agreed in his blog, saying: "Firstly, the Tories wouldn't want him! Secondly he wouldn't want them!"[13]

However, I wonder if Ian has been in Eastbourne- and its unusual political balance- just a bit too long ? In other parts of the country, the Lib Dems are quite happy to make up the numbers in formal coalition (or wobbly deals) with the Tories on local councils- Hastings being an example.

Stung by criticism that he is just "Cameron-lite", Clegg has taken to turning this around, and accused David Cameron of trying to be "Clegg-lite" Cameron does indeed describe himself again and again as being a "liberal" Conservative.

Labour supporters should let them get on with their "how-liberal-are-you ?" love-in, and get on with campaigning for the only alternative to Cameron (0r Cameron-Clegg-Coallition): A fourth-term Labour government.

Saturday, 1 March 2008
OFFICIAL: Lib Dems not allowed opinion

Lib Dem foreign affairs spokesman Ed Davey being sent for an early bath by the Deputy Speaker, for continuous rowdy interruptions, made good TV, but a look at the background to the case tells you all you need to know about the Lib Dems.

Davey's fit of pique was caused by the decision not to grant the Lib Dems a debate on their proposal for a referendum on withdrawing from the EU.

The Lib Dems are the most consistently pro-European of the three main parties. They wholeheartedly support British membership of the EU and the signing of the Lisbon Treaty.

So why are they asking for a referendum on leaving the EU ? Well, precisely because they don't want to alienate their raft of soft-Tory supporters by coming across as being (gasp) too pro-Europe. They are banking on the fact that the majority of people would realise that to withdraw from the EU altogether would be an economic disaster for Britain, with so much trade and so many jobs depending on it.

The "in or out" referendum proposal give them a perfect get-out for any debate about the rights and wrongs of the constitution/treaty or any other detailed element of EU policy.

Dominic Lawson's excellent column in yesterday's Independent seized on Nick Clegg's habit of talking in metaphors ("Genghis" described the Speaker's decision on his amendment as "like allowing the British public to choose their mode of travel without asking whether they actually want to continue on the journey at all.") Lawson replies with a metaphor of his own: "Imagine you are at a restaurant with some friends, sharing the bill. You have all eaten two courses and are now discussing whether to order some pudding. Suddenly one diner says that the debate should actually be about whether it was a mistake to have eaten the previous dishes. When he is politely told not to be so silly by his companions, he walks out of the restaurant. This, it seems to me, is a reasonable description of the Liberal Democrats' behaviour as they stagily stalked out of the House of Commons" [14]

So, having committed his Party to such an odd policy position, how will "Genghis" Clegg hold his troops in line ? With a rod of orange iron, that's how. He has threatened that if any of his front bench vote at all in the debate on the Lisbon treaty, they will be dismissed. Yep, you heard. If a Lib Dem MP has the temerity to express an opinion on the treaty, or to cast his vote in what he believes to be his constituents' best interests, he will be sacked.

e-Politix almost named Alistair Carmichael -Lib Dem spokesman on Northern Ireland- as a potential rebel (i.e. they thought he might express an opinion on this major issue), but it seems that may just have been wishful thinking. As the statements were all made in Lib-Demese, I haven't yet had a chance to translate them into English. This is what Carmichael told e-Politix. See if you can work it out:

"It remains to be seen exactly how things unfold next week - it will surprise nobody that I am not going to commit myself one way or the other just yet because we don't yet know what is going to be on the order paper and what we will be asked to vote on." [15]

So is he prepared to risk the sack for his principles ???

"If we proceed on the basis that we are all acting according to our own lights and with good will and good faith then whatever the outcome is at the end of the day I am fairly hopeful that whatever differences we may have as a party we will still come through it as a fairly united force."

That's....er...clear then.

Sunday, 20 July 2008
She's not dead yet, Gordon...

Am I the only one who thinks it's a **bit sick** talking about somebody's funeral before they've shuffled off this mortal coil ? Never mind the **inappropriateness** of Thatcher being given the honour of a State Funeral previously only afforded to Royalty (*although Thatcher sometimes got confused about that...*) and five non-Royals: **Nelson, Wellington, Palmerston, Gladstone and Winston Churchill.**

Churchill had an input into his own celebrations- but, of course, as the **Man who Won the War** it was taken as read that there would be a state funeral. The Old Man, allegedly, made the request that his funeral train should depart from **Waterloo Station**, and then change at Reading, en route to his familial home at Blenheim. When organisers protested, he clarified that if **General De Gaulle** died first, then the train could depart from anywhere. But, if the General was to be present, then it would depart from Waterloo...

But even he did not have the indignity of his funeral arrangements subjected to **public debate** in the tabloids. The late Queen Mother had a comprehensive funeral plan drawn up some years before her death at 101. I was reliably informed by a military friend that this package had the codename: "Operation Hope Not."

Certainly, Thatcher should have a public **memorial service**: as afforded to many figures in public life. One of my first tasks as a Labour Party member was to represent the Eastbourne Constituency at the Westminster Abbey service of remembrance for **John Smith**. My late general secretary **Steve Sinnott** was recently honoured by many public figures, including Ed Balls and the Tory front bench spokesman at the QEII Conference Centre.

But a State funeral- including, one assumes, the public **lying-in-state of the coffin** ? Even Blair- who was not adverse to praising the nemesis of the Labour movement- ruled that out[16]. Apart from the fact that Maggie's dad Alderman Roberts would probably turn in his own grave (as a **Methodist** lay minister he was not a fan of the adornments, trappings and rituals of the High Church) why should Maggie be treated any differently to our other former Prime Ministers ?

- **She won three general elections**: So did Blair, and I doubt very much he would qualify. Harold Wilson won four.

- **She brought about massive social change**: Yep- some of which destroyed industries, communities and ushered in an era of exploitation and disillusionment of working people. In any case, look at how Thatcher's achievements compare to those of **Attlee**, who gave us the NHS, or **Heath** who took us into the European Union (yes…. I know…but certainly a significant event...) and neither of these was given such an honour.
- **She won the Cold War**: A bit disingenuous to the likes of Solidarity or those who booed Ceausescu. Does Gorbachev receive no credit? Jim Callaghan before her was no friend of the Communists. Also, if we are holding up Thatcher as a paragon of international stateswomanship, isn't it **ironic** that, when the world celebrates the 90th birthday of **Nelson Mandela**, we are talking about an honour for the woman who refused sanctions against apartheid South Africa, and branded Nelson Mandela a **terrorist** ? (*Young Conservatives in the 1980's wore T-shirts with the slogan* **"Hang Nelson Mandela"** *Some of these people are now Tory MPs*) .
- **She was our first woman Prime Minister**: Yes- very important and significant, and ensuring her place in the history books for ever. That fact certainly should indeed be celebrated, but in an appropriate way. Does her gender alone give a reason for such an extravagant send off?

Some **cynics** suggest that the announcement of the Thatcher State Funeral was a ruse to **divert attention** from domestic political issues. If it was, then it's in **pretty poor taste**, and unlikely to endear Gordon Brown to the core voters who he needs to keep motivated (not least in Glasgow East where massive unemployment and an early Poll Tax did not make Thatcher a particularly popular figure.)

Thatcher is reported to be in **good health**, and a mere 82 years old (my Nan is 100 next month, by the way,) so it is unlikely that Gordon will need to make the decision. However, by opening this rather morbid can of worms, this is now likely to become, (in the words of those insurance policy adverts) a "whole of life" debate. A pity.

HEALTH

The NHS. Indisputably the greatest achievement of the 1945 Labour government, and still a talisman to those on the progressive wing of British politics. While it stands against the instincts of the Conservative Party, no Tory government has ever seriously challenged the concept of healthcare free for all (although some in the headier days of the Thatcher government speculated...)

My local Conservative MEP, Daniel Hannam, has become a darling of the Right on American television, with a special line in NHS-bashing, calling it a "60 year mistake." How safe is the NHS if extremists like Hannam get control of the Tories? More importantly, can the Labour government step up to defend the NHS, and avoid own-goals like the defeated proposals to cut services at Eastbourne's hospital. These columns explore...

Saturday, 30 June 2007
My new favourite MP ?

It sounds unlikely, but my least-favourite Deputy Leadership candidate could turn his standing with me and many other teachers and public servants around, by getting to grips with the looming hospital closures or "downgrades" in the NHS.

Johnson must be smarting after losing the deputy leadership by less than 1%, and needs a big public success to build his popularity (and restore his wounded self-esteem!) His job as Health Secretary could be just the tonic....

For readers not living in this neck of the woods, the NHS is a pretty big issue on the doorstep. Our local hospital, Eastbourne DGH has been under a shadow for more than a year, with the NHS Trust threatening a number of cuts. At one stage, the A&E department was threatened with downgrade to a "minor injury unit", although common sense has prevailed here (it's a long and congested road to Hastings.)

Still under threat, however, are maternity / specialist baby care services. All of the trust's models are build around either Eastbourne DGH or Hastings' Conquest Hospital having their specialist services reduced to midwife led delivery rooms only, or, in some models, no labour facilities at all.

Eastbourne folk are not traditionally militant, but this has got them going. The Save the DGH campaign has been a cross-party campaign (although Tory MP Nigel Waterson has been accused of lifting petition signatures to send them "vote Tory" letters) and the campaign has been heavily pushing a fifth option, "Option 5 Saves Lives", which is different to the official 4 suggested by the trust, and keeps consultant-led services at both hospitals.

The NHS trust has operated in deficit, and argues that the cuts must be made for financial reasons. The government has, up until now, been adopting a firm "no blank cheque" approach to those trusts with financial problems.

Trouble is, despite the impression occasionally given- the NHS is NOT a business, it is a public service. A hospital cannot be allowed to go bust, cut services or be asset stripped. Like schools, they have to be in place to serve local communities.

(Deep breath)..... Alan Johnson could learn some lessons from his time at DfES, by looking at how OFSTED deal with schools in serious weaknesses....(grits teeth some more.) If a school is deemed to be failing, the local authority can come in and directly run the school- sorting out problems and, usually, getting rid of management who have been found wanting. True, OFSTED can close schools, but usually re-open them under a new name, with new management, and a financial fresh start.

How about the same for NHS Trusts who have cocked-up the books ? Get rid of the management, sort out areas of weakness, and then send them off on a clean footing. The "hit squad" would have to be given an agenda of clinical need (so doctors and medical experts should outweigh and outvote the accountants !) frontline staff and services should be protected, and, once management and accounting systems have been put in place, yes- the government should write off debts incurred by the former trust, as local people should not be punished for incompetent managers.

Will Alan Johnson intervene to "Save the DGH?" It would be a bold step, and would need to be repeated in other parts of the country, but it would back up Gordon Brown's assertion that Health is his "number one priority." Get this right, and, far from the spectacle of his predecessor being heckled by the uber-moderate Royal College of Nurses, Alan Johnson could become the toast of the NHS. Next time there's a deputy leadership election, I might even vote for him...

Sunday, 26 August 2007
A sign of the times ?

I found myself reflecting on how as times change, so do our values. The inspiration for this bit of moral reflection? Visiting my friend, vice-chair, and often running mate in Hampden Park, Ann Ring.

Ann has not been well these last few months, and, regrettably had to stay a few nights in hospital. As I was at Sainsbury's- I dropped by into the DGH to see her- a visit costing me £1.70 (more for longer stays)

Hospital parking charges are an old story, politically. It is a good few years ago that Eastbourne, along with most others, introduced these charges, initially to pay for the upkeep of the car parks- now to help raise funds for the good work of the hospital.

However, something still grates with me. How many people like me drop in to see friends ? How often has a friend, whose visit will have cheered up somebody's afternoon, found that they haven't got any change, and decided to give it a miss ? Are we so "economically correct" as a society that we can't give every encouragement possible to citizens to go and support their neighbours when they are unwell ?

More worryingly in recent months:-

Volunteers from religious communities no longer get free parking. With local people following scores of different faiths and denominations, the counsel of a faith leader is incredibly comforting and supportive for people in times of sickness. Colin Belsey, (a Tory councillor, and Nigel Waterson's assistant, so not somebody I agree with often) said, quite rightly to the Herald: "I find it extraordinary that a pastor has to pay for the privilege of saying a few prayers to the patients," while the minster of the central Methodist Church gave a far more stark observation: "If you are sitting with someone who is dying you cannot keeping running out to fill up the parking meter." [2]

From the end of last year, STAFF in the hospital have been charged 50p per day to park. Hospital managers put a green sheen on this policy, suggesting that it is an "incentive for staff to leave their car at home" and stating that their staff support "Healthy Transport" while recognising that this (stealthy reclaiming of wages) will also generate £200,000 for the trust[3].
I accept the balance sheet reality of our hospitals, and in no way is this any sort of policy pledge from me or from the Labour Party, but on a purely

personal level, I find myself asking is this what the NHS was supposed to be about ? The great socialist achievement of the 1945 Labour government, that no Tory government would ever dream of privatising. Nye Bevan envisaged the NHS as being at the heart of our then commitment to cradle-to-grave welfare. (Bevan resigned over the imposition of charges for glasses and dentures- he must be spinning in his grave now!)

I'm not (ever on this blog) going to talk about tax commitments- knowing how destructive they become in any election campaign. But perhaps if Gordon Brown's suggestion of a more independent NHS management comes true, that new politically-independent management can factor into their funding requests real issues of patient comfort and dignity (including the right to visits from family members and spiritual advisers: the Human Rights Act mentions both !)

Rare moment of Utopianism from me- I'm sure I'll be back to normal next time !

Sunday, 23 December 2007
The fight goes on

One afternoon in November, I had to drive to speak to a teachers' meeting in a Hastings school. I left Ratton at 3.20pm, before the rush hour had really kicked in, and arrived (after a minute stop to phone in my apologies for lateness half way) at 4.30pm. My journey was not life threatening, fortunately, but had I been transporting an expectant mother with serious complications, it could have been a different story.

The Primary Care Trust voted by 11 to 3 to close consultant led maternity services and the special care baby unit at the DGH, under the gross misapprehension that this service could be provided at the Conquest Hospital in Hastings.

The *Save the DGH* campaign and the *Hands Off the Conquest* have been campaigning tirelessly for months to stop this happening. The campaign has been supported by all parties, and has been resolute in resisting any temptation to "rob Peter to pay Paul"- both campaigns insist that both units be maintained.

The PCT seems to have some odd reasoning. They maintain that the unit will be accessible within the NICE stipulation that emergency cases must be treated within 75 minutes (try doing the journey at the height of rush hour.)

They claim that Hastings, with its higher levels of social deprivation need the unit more, because: "there was very strong evidence linking levels of deprivation and premature births. Women in deprived areas were five times more likely to have problems with birth" Very true, but that simply proves that we need a unit in Hastings- it doesn't follow that because Eastbourne mothers are better off on average that they won't suffer from birthing problems that will be made far worse by a 75 minutes plus ambulance journey!

The hospital campaigners were not simply being oppositionalist. The Option 5 (which they had to fight to get included in the public consultation) kept both units open, was costed and practical, and recognised the need to develop a centre of regional excellence at Brighton for the most seriously ill babies. This cut no ice with the faceless bureaucrats on the PCT.

So where now ?

Eastbourne (and Hastings) GPs have the opportunity to call a vote of "no confidence" in the PCT board. They must now do this.

There is discussion of a judicial review. Do the figures for travel times to Hastings really meet the NICE standards? Were the public really listened to in the "consultation" ?

Most importantly, we need Alan Johnson to get his hands dirty on this one. The line has consistently been that this is a locally devolved decision, and is not for the Secretary of State to interfere with. However, he does have the power to intervene if a PCT is acting recklessly or perversely. This decision clearly goes against medical wisdom, local feeling and good common sense.

The Labour Party created the NHS. Nye Bevan isn't around anymore, but the Welsh hero was never afraid of taking on the powerful establishments. Alan Johnson needs to do the same.

Saturday 14 July 2007
Hastings Councillors bottle it...

I was as dismayed as almost every other Eastbourne resident to read that the Cabinet of Hastings Borough Council have seemingly bottled out of the fight to retain maternity services in both of our towns. The cabinet voted instead to back "Option 4," which would preserve the unit at the Conquest in Hastings and close the facility at Eastbourne DGH.

Tory Councillor Matthew Lock (the "genius" behind the parking scheme imposed by East Sussex on the unwilling people of Eastbourne) justified his decision by saying:

"I was elected as a councillor by the people of Hastings, so I'm happy to back what's best for Hastings. I was not elected by the people of Eastbourne." [1]

This simple, selfish creature does not seem to recognise that he is playing into the hands of the Primary Care Trust, who will be delighted that they have succeeded with the council where they resolutely failed with the grass-roots campaigners, with a blatant divide-and-rule tactic.

Both the Save the DGH campaign and the Conquest Hospital group have consistently backed a two-hospital approach- promoting the Option 5- Saves Lives campaign that would keep both units open. Now, by drawing the short-sighted Hastings Councillors into backing a "me-first" approach, they will doubtless expect Eastbourne's political leaders to back the opposite option, thus cancelling each other out and letting the PCT press on with whatever their preferred option is saying, with mock sympathy, "Well, there was no consensus between the towns."

I hope that both campaigns, which include all political parties and many non-political local people from both towns, are not drawn in to the rob-Peter-to-pay-Paul approach, and stand firm on this issue. We can still make the Hastings Councillors' decision stand out for what it is- out of touch, unrepresentative and irrelevant. Option 5 is the antithesis to Matthew Lock's glib statement- it is not about what's "best" for one side only- it is about what's RIGHT- and in the long term, that will benefit both towns.

Come on Alan Johnson- get your hands dirty!

Sunday 3 February 2008
Mr Lock and LOCAL democracy

My letter, published in the Eastbourne Herald this weekend:-

"Eastbourne seems to occupy a lot of Hastings Tory councillor Matthew Lock's time and energy. This is the man who is the brain (?) behind the unwanted parking scheme that the County Council continues to try and foist on Eastbourne. With recent talks ending in deadlock, Cllr Lock has the power to impose the scheme, and last week's comments suggest he will do exactly that, regardless of the wishes of Eastbourne residents.

Last year, while the DGH and Conquest Hospital campaigners stood shoulder to shoulder to oppose cuts at either facility, Matthew Lock broke the solidarity between the people of our towns, by voting in favour of the Hastings option, stating bluntly: 'I was not elected by the people of Eastbourne.' Have we done something to upset him ?" [4]

It poses an interesting question about the role of Borough and County Councils, and the relationship between the two systems. As an NUT official, working with East Sussex County Council on a regular basis, I would strongly defend the County's role in Education. Clearly the size of the service, and the needs of advisory, personnel and legal support, School Improvement Services, music service, behaviour support etc. etc. mean that an authority the size of Eastbourne Borough would not be able to provide the range of support and expertise required.

At the other end of the spectrum comes the question of on-street parking. Is this really a strategic decision that needs a county-wide vision ? The variety of schemes in different parts of East Sussex do not suggest that there is any sort of "vision" for parking across the county ! It is absolutely right that road transport issues are the prerogative of ESCC- indeed, there needs to be more "joined up" thinking between authorities to create coherent transport policy. But how is whether we have parking meters and how much we charge in our town centre any business of a Tory cabinet in Lewes (who do not, incidentally, have a single cabinet member from Eastbourne ?)

At the risk of sounding like a Lib Dem, I have always believed in devolving power to the lowest appropriate level. By allowing a puffed up Hastings Tory to make decisions that properly belong to the people of Eastbourne and their local representatives does not strike me as the best example of local democracy in action…

Sunday, 3 February 2008
TRAITOR

Barry Taylor is one of the luckiest Tories in Eastbourne. As a long-serving member from Meads (although he got lucky when long-serving Tory councillor Aubrey Vickers unexpectedly resigned in the 1990's- creating the by-election that ushered him in) Barry Taylor represents the only ward in Eastbourne never to have elected an opposition councilor- one of the few parts of Eastbourne left where still "they don't count the Tory vote, they weigh it."

Has the power gone to his head ? Because, after all of the work done by the Save the DGH campaign, including Nigel Waterson MP and Ian Lucas, he has stabbed them all in the back.

The Health Overview Scrutiny Committee for East Sussex was the last great hope for the DGH campaign. By rejecting the PCT proposals (which it did, although 3 councillors voted to support it- read on...) the decision now goes back to the Secretary of State's desk. I have written to Dawn Primarolo on behalf of Eastbourne Labour, urging a rethink. Barry Taylor, on the other hand, elected by the people of Meads, supported by Nigel Waterson, promoted to cabinet by Ian Lucas, cast his vote IN SUPPORT OF ENDING MATERNITY AT THE DGH.

The DGH is full of men (and women) in white coats. So, I am reminded of the original political man in a white suit, Martin Bell. He was the journalist who stood against disgraced Tory MP Neil Hamilton in rock-solid Tatton, and defeated him on an anti-sleaze platform. Unlike Barry Taylor, Neil Hamilton's disgraceful behaviour didn't threaten the safety, if not the lives, of mothers and unborn children. Maybe that is what Meads now needs?

So, here's a thought. Although we've got to wait until May 2009, people in Eastbourne have long memories. Let's make Barry Taylor's County Council Seat (the reason he was on the HOSC committee in the first place) a referendum on maternity services at the DGH. If the (usually supine) Meads Tories reselect this public health traitor for those elections, I will propose to my party that we do not fight the ward. I will ask the Lib Dems and the Greens to do the same. Then, let's find someone genuinely independent, knowledgeable about the NHS and public health, and persuade them to stand in Meads. How comfy will Barry Taylor's majority feel then ???

Wednesday, 5 March 2008
Getting it right in the valleys

It's not often that I find myself in agreement with the *Daily Mail*- but on the issue of hospital parking charges (I gave my own opinion on these way back in August) we are in full accord.

The Welsh Assembly has approved the scrapping of car parking charges in NHS hospitals in Wales. The response from the DoH in England has been the rather predictable: it is not in line with the Government's environmental policy aims.

Yes- we all need to do our bit to stave of climate change, but it is absolute folly to say that car park charges will make people more likely to walk or take the bus to hospital. Many of the folks paying to park will be bringing others to appointments who are not feeling up to a long walk, others (as I was) will be dropping in on friends or relatives. Some in Eastbourne will be religious or faith leaders since the DGH ended free passes for these people who give so much comfort and support to the sick.

There is a delicate balance between encouraging people to drive less, and recognising that we are currently a car-using society. I continue to maintain that our hospitals are not the ideal place to try and alter people's environmental behaviour ! The Mail article quotes a spokesman from doctors' trade union, the BMA as saying:

"It is completely unacceptable for hospitals to charge extortionate fees for car parking, which does nothing more than penalize patients when they are most in need."

Well done to unions like the BMA and Royal College of Nursing, and the Macmillan Cancer charity for the pressure they continue to exert on this issue.

The Welsh Assembly has a record of putting forward progressive policies that Westminster could do well to follow (scrapping school league tables, etc.) So Llongyfarchion to my Labour colleagues in Wales- let's hope it's an idea which catches on....

Saturday 24 May 2008
Outbreak of Common Sense

The campaign to save consultant-led maternity services at the DGH continues apace, with Liz Walke's courageous decision to head up a legal challenge. The focus of the campaign is now on raising the estimated £150,000 needed to allow that to happen.

May 9th saw a Day of Action for the campaign- with Nigel Waterson and Lib Dem council leader David Tutt putting aside their differences for the day and travelling around Eastbourne collecting money and sponsorship.

I was pleased to lend my support to Liz and the team at the Rodmill in the evening, where they rounded off with a live outside broadcast on Sovereign Radio.

I was interviewed for Labour's point of view on the campaign by top local radio presenter Ryan Millns, and I was happy once again to give our full backing to the campaign. Ryan asked me what would solve the problem, and I was able to suggest "an outbreak of common sense", for that is the crux of the issue. If the faceless bureaucrats got off their backsides and talked to people, and maybe tried to do the road journey from Eastbourne to Hastings (imagining themselves in the role of a soon-to-be mum) then there would be no further need for debate!

Liz needs as many people to lobby the Independent Reconfiguration Panel to get the decision reversed (if that is successful then we won't need our day in court!) Liz has circulated the following request, which I am happy to print in full:

"As you probably know, the Save the DGH Campaign were delighted that East Sussex County Council Health Overview and Scrutiny Committee were not happy with the decision to downgrade Eastbourne Maternity Unit and have referred the matter to the Secretary of State for Health, Alan Johnson, to review the decision made by our local Primary Care Trust (PCT).

The Secretary of State for Health has decided that the matter requires a full review and has passed it on to the Independent Reconfiguration Panel (IRP).

During a full review the IRP will consider whether proposed changes to health services will ensure the provision of safe, sustainable and accessible services for local people. The focus of all reviews is the patient and quality of care. As part of the review process the IRP considers written evidence, makes site visits and gathers information from all interested parties.

Following collection of evidence the IRP will submit a report containing recommendations to the Health Secretary. The IRP provides advice only. The final decisions on changes will be made by the Health Secretary. Last week there was a letter in the local papers from Dr Peter Barrett, Chair of the IPR asking for local people to give their views and give information that was not submitted or heard during the consultation process."

Sunday, 7 September 2008
SAVED the DGH !

I've given health (and former education) secretary Alan Johnson a bit of a hard time in this column over the last few months: indeed in the very first entry, regarding the Labour deputy leadership contest, I opined that I would chew my own arm off before I'd vote for him to take that position. However, a few weeks later, I asked the question "Could Alan Johnson be my Favourite MP ?" in which I urged him to intervene and save consultant led maternity services at the DGH.

Well, it took a long time, a lot of sweat, campaigning and lobbying, but Alan Johnson has upheld the recommendation of the Independent Reconfiguration Panel and declared that the service must stay at the DGH.

The Save the DGH Campaign has WON !

This would not have been possible without the determination and energy of the Save the DGH campaign, led by **Liz Walke** and **Monica Corrina-Kavakli**, and supported by political and community leaders from all parties.

CONGRATULATIONS TO:
- **Liz**, **Monica** and all the activists in the campaign
- **Richard and Liz Goude** who represented Eastbourne Labour Party on the campaign team.
- **Nigel Waterson MP**, Ian Lucas and most of the Tory councillors (not Barry Taylor, borough and county councillor for Meads- see earlier article on his voting record...)
- **David Tutt**, Norman Baker MP, Stephen Lloyd and the Lib Dems on Eastbourne Borough Council.
- **Dr John Clarke**, consultant **Vincent Argent**, and the **Eastbourne GPs** for their unstinting support
- **Labour MP** for Hastings, Mike Foster, and the dedicated team from the **Hands off the Conquest Hospital** campaign. They could have stopped campaigning after the Hastings unit was saved, but showed their principles and integrity by never wavering from their support for Eastbourne's fight.
- and.. above all... the thousands of Eastbourne residents who marched, lobbied, wrote letters and e-mails and fundraised superbly. **This was Eastbourne's fight, and Eastbourne's victory.**

Alan Johnson, of course, did spend an awful lot of time thinking about the situation- taking advice from the PCT (who wanted to close it), the local Health Overview Scrutiny Committee (most of whom wanted to save it- see earlier post..) Eastbourne Council (who wanted to keep both units open), Hastings Council (who only wanted to save Hastings…) and finally the Independent Reconfiguration Panel. But, eventually, the **correct decision** was made.

My application for the Alan Johnson fan club is ready to be posted (not sure where I put my stamps...) but, perhaps Alan will be more pleased by the tribute from **Lewes' Lib Dem MP Norman Baker**, who said:
"Well done Alan Johnson. It is good to see that there is at least one Minister who is listening to the public.[6]"

**Congratulations again to EVERYBODY who made this possible.
Eastbourne is a town that can be proud of itself !**

EDUCATION EDUCATION EDUCATION

As a teacher, Education is both a political and a personal passion. When I started writing the column, I was also a Union representative at my school- by the end of the column's first life, I had risen to be Secretary of the National Union of Teachers in East Sussex, and a member of the union's National Executive committee. These columns look at the issues that faced teachers and children during that time.

Monday, 9 July 2007
Officially a NUT

Saturday morning was a special day for me, as I was officially appointed as the Divisional (County) Secretary for the National Union of Teachers. This means I will be responsible for co-ordinating the work of the union across the county, and especially with getting reps and members actively involved in the smaller schools.

I have been an NUT member for all of my teaching career, and support the union's education policies fully. This makes for some interesting discussions with Labour Party colleagues about some upcoming issues:

"The union is threatening action over the 2% pay offer:" Good. I will support it. Teachers' pay has markedly improved since 1997, but, in the same way that boom and bust is dangerous for the economy, it is a real problem for teachers and their families in terms of keeping up with living costs. Many teachers have mortgages that may be affected by the interest rate rise, while council tax and other bills have risen beyond inflation. Add to that inflation which, in reality has been knocking around the 4% mark, and what you actually have is a pay CUT of 2% on the table. It is important that we also support claims by Unison and other public sector unions, whose members are in the same position, but, with many members on lower salaries, will be harder hit in terms of the affect on their standard of living.

"The union is opposed to the flagship Academies project:" So am I. I believe in state education, and, for that to succeed it needs to be based on a good local school for every child. Academies not only drain resources that could be used to improve many local schools, but, in handing over to business leaders, exclude parents, staff and local communities from having any real say in the governance of the school. The groups involved in the current Academies also include a number of very dubious evangelical Christian fundamentalists, who threaten the provision of a genuinely broad based and questioning curriculum. Anybody doubting me, should buy a copy of Francis Beckett's book *The Great City Academy Fraud*.

"Teachers are becoming increasingly anti-Labour:" Not sure if this is true- there's certainly very little enthusiasm for the Tories. The record investment by the government in education is more than welcome. Teachers are, however disenchanted by the sheer weight of policy initiative after policy initiative that has come out from the government in recent years. We need time to settle and embed changes, and for policy to be rooted in the fact

that teachers are professionals who are usually the best people to make decisions about children's education.

The government has excluded the NUT (biggest teachers union in Europe) from the "social partnership", which includes the smaller unions, including scab union PAT.: Yes, and that's a disgrace. It makes a mockery of our belief in trade unionism, especially as, in the average local Labour Party, NUT members are aplenty, while you will be lucky to find a single member of any of the other unions (especially PAT)

The election of Gordon Brown is a chance for a fresh start between the NUT and the government. However, I shall be constantly aware that the NUT is politically independent, and I shall campaign to implement the policy of the union. I shall be doing my best to persuade the Party of which I have been a member of for nearly 14 years to listen to teachers, take note and act accordingly!

Friday, 7 September 2007
Cameron: Bottom of the Class

You know that Summer is officially over on that day when the roads suddenly start to clog at about 8.15am- yep- the school run is back, and so are the kids !

Having started back in the classroom this week, it seems like a good time to talk about education- and some good news.

The Labour government's pilot project **Making Good Progress** will see more than 50 schools in East Sussex receive extra funding to allow children identified as falling behind, the opportunity of receiving 10 hours of one-to-one tuition in addition to their school time. This has to be delivered by a properly paid and fully qualified teacher. Schools and teachers (the division is being negotiated !) will receive cash bonuses if that child makes significant progress as a result of the extra intervention.

Progress will be tested by a single-level standard assessment that can be delivered at the appropriate time (ie. after a period of intervention) - a model which, if successful, could pave the way to it replacing the flawed SAT at 14, and, in the process provide a much more accurate and useful picture of a child's progress. Compare this needs-led, child focused policy on the absolutely barmy proposal of the Tories'- to keep under achieving students back in Primary school.

Children are developing rapidly, both physically and emotionally at 11. They are all geared up to moving to "big school" and a different, age-appropriate working environment. Do these Tory "experts" really think that keeping a child in junior school- marking them out in the most highly visible way (all of their friends seeing them in their old "little school" uniform for a start) is going to help them develop into well adjusted and happy youngsters ? Do they really think that keeping them in an environment where they are surrounded by younger and smaller children will help them develop age-appropriate social skills and working habits ? For that matter, what is the effect going to be on the other students in the Primary school, having a bigger, disillusioned and probably very angry older student or students in their class ?

Frankly, the whole tone of the Tory policy seems to celebrate the "stigmatisation" element; implying that children will somehow work harder because of the threat of such a dire and damaging punishment.

I am not a fan of the systems (such as the USA) where this policy already happens. I don't think is best for our kids. I do not believe it is either morally or educationally valid to punish children as young as 11 for apparently underachieving.

Children who are not reaching their potential need positive, professional and focused intervention to support them. That means small class or even one-to-one help, tailored to their needs, and delivered by experts, in an environment that builds their confidence, esteem and self-respect rather than belittling it. It has nothing to do with which phase of school the child is in- it is to do with funding and resourcing all schools to enable projects such as Making Good Progress to make a difference.

Sunday, 17 February 2008
Corporals in class ?

Has school discipline got so bad that we need to call in the army ? No, despite what some people may tell you, my colleagues and I do not live in fear of our students. In fact, I can safely say that in six years in the secondary classroom, I have never felt any fear for my physical safety.

In some schools, especially inner city areas, this is not always the case, and schools have installed equipment such as metal detectors to prevent knives being brought in. A sad sign of the times, but still, in the main, a preventative measure to keep our schools safe places for students and teachers.

So, I was interested to read about the *Troops to Teach* project being floated as an option for this country[1]. Already, the USA has a well established programme, encouraging and training retiring or retired military personnel to take up posts as school teachers.

I have a lot of respect for the skills that are learned by people who choose careers in the armed services, and many of them already go on to civilian careers as teachers (my father was one of them !) But I am cautious about importing a US system that appears to reinforce the wholly false assumption that our kids are out of control in school and need a boot-camp atmosphere to bring them into line. I have said it a hundred times, and I will say it again- most of our kids behave well and work hard at school.

I even found myself in the uncomfortable position of agreeing with Chris Keates of the NASUWT union- who commented:

"The project also seems to be based on a flawed premise that teaching is simply crowd control. Promoting the concept that boys only respond to tough male role models is insulting to the thousands of women teachers who maintain high standards of classroom discipline through their skill and professionalism."[2]

(I giggled that this came from the leader of a union that was initially set up as an all-male union to oppose equal pay for women teachers, but 30-odd years on from them finally letting women in, I suppose I can let that drop…)

Education benefits hugely from the numbers of teachers who train for the profession later in life, having followed a first career. The diverse range of skills that they bring from the "outside world" is invaluable to any school. So we shouldn't throw resources into trying to recruit from just one source, but promote and enhance the status of the education professions (not helped by imposed three-year pay cuts, incidentally Gordon)

So come on Gordon and Ed - we don't just need soldiers- we need talented and committed people from all backgrounds who value our young people and care about education- to train to join the hundreds of thousands of teachers and support staff who already do this fantastic job !

Sunday, 6 April 2008
RIP: Steve Sinnott (1951-2008)

Steve Sinnott was the General Secretary of the National Union of Teachers- my union. His sudden and totally unexpected death yesterday has shocked not just the union, but the whole education community to the core.

Steve was a passionate and committed fighter for education- both in Britain and across the world. I first met Steve when he was Deputy General Secretary, at an event talking about education in Latin America. Steve was known as a passionate internationalist- if we believe in education as a fundamental human right, that has to go beyond any national boundaries. He kept that internationalism as he assumed the top job in the Union.

Like any democratic organisation, the NUT has its internal differences. Steve worked tirelessly throughout his time at the helm to promote unity and agreement- and the united conference I attended in Manchester showed that he had made considerable strides to achieve that.

Steve's formidable intellect, media savvy and scouse charm were a huge asset in the build up to the National Strike on 24th April- Steve stood out as an articulate and amiable advocate for our cause, often against immense media provocation.

I last spoke to Steve on Tuesday, at the national Executive meeting of the union, that voted unanimously to take national action. Steve spoke passionately and thoughtfully, answering all manner of awkward questions, and demonstrating he was ready to lead us in this most regrettable action with energy and vigour. I can't believe that he's gone.

My thoughts, and those of all in the education community, are with Mary and Steve's children and grandchildren.

Thursday, 27 March 2008
Lies, damned lies and the Daily Express

I spent my Easter weekend in enjoyable discussion, debate and networking with more than a thousand other teachers at the annual conference of the National Union of Teachers. A broad and entirely relevant range of topics was covered- inclusion, class sizes, support for early years, pressure facing young teachers, curriculum reform, behaviour etc: all subjects that you would expect a group of highly committed professionals to be interested in.

The issue of faith schools is one that most teachers have an opinion about. Currently the postcode lottery of school places is compounded by children of Church of England or Catholic worshippers being able to jump to the head of the respective queues for what are perceived as "better" schools. In some parts of the country, Muslim parents, quite understandably, are keen to see state schools that reflect their faith in the same way (there are already a number of Islamic and Jewish state schools, as well as hundreds of CofE and Catholic ones.) Opponents worry that this will artificially segregate multi-ethnic areas, and will work against goals of bringing about community cohesion.

My Union set up a working party that took hours of oral evidence and written submissions from teachers, faith leaders and secular organisations. The report was the result of much discussion and debate, and amongst other things recognised that many parents wish for their children to be instructed in the tenets of their religion, and that it was preferable to allow for this to be an optional part of the curriculum in a comprehensive school, rather than through segregated faith schools.

How did the Daily Express interpret this balanced and scholarly report ?[3] How do you think ? Another opportunity to use the "Muslim Extremist" line to whip up fear. The fact that the motions on faith schools were never reached in the agenda owing to time pressures, so were not even discussed at the conference did not get in the way of a good story.

From it's fairly liberal leanings under Rosie Boycott a few years ago, the Express has now become an organ of the far right: proprietor Richard Desmond (until recently owner of the top-shelf magazines Big Ones, Skinny and Wriggly, Posh Housewives and Asian Babes) now has an entirely new type of filth to peddle. (The Express cemented its reputation as a purveyor of its own unique brand of "truth" earlier this month, when it paid the McCanns £550,000 after publishing more than 100 defamatory articles about them.)

Aside from the Express' take on the conference, I suppose I ought to give a few thoughts of my own on the Faith School debate. On principle I am against faith schools- I think that segregating pupils on the basis of parents denominational faith is utterly wrong, and, in many mixed areas is likely to foment distrust (Northern Ireland's school system remains heavily divided- although it was worse in the past !) Moreover, many churches (particularly CofE) see an influx of school-place tourists for a few years for the purposes of getting their children into the right school. As a Christian, I am uncomfortable about such material enticements to swell church congregations...

No government is going to propose abolition of Faith Schools, as any party would suffer heavily as a result. The "freedom of choice" argument is well applied to this difficult debate. However, I believe there is a solution....

Politicians and parents alike cite the "ethos" of the faith schools as a reason for sending their kids there (as against the more middle-class and higher than average academic ability of the students getting in...) and I think that there is some truth in that, although a lot is in perception. A catholic comrade explained to me that she wanted her children to go to Catholic school because "the discipline was good, and they're not allowed to swear". Funnily enough, they're not allowed to swear or misbehave in my state comprehensive either, although the faith schools clearly have the ability to enforce this more rigorously with practically universal parental support for the school across the board, and less restrictions on exclusion.

The schools, in turn, claim that they are not about segregation or sectarianism, but exist to support and nurture the gift of education for all. (Historically, the churches were providing free or cheap schools for the poor long before the State got involved.) So, to me, the answer is clear:

Keep the church schools open, but get rid of the "worshipping parent" requirement to get a place.

If parents want their child to go to a well resourced (ie. normal state funding, topped up by the church) school with an ethos rooted in faith based values, then let them choose. But open the places to all, using a fair admissions policy. It would upset a few key churches, who will not be able to swell their congregations and coffers with hopeful parents- but maybe they will have to go back to the community work and evangelism that many other churches rely on.

To finish, I feel I ought to mention a school in this constituency that sits as a beacon against the segregated faith school argument. Ocklynge School in Old Town is a huge junior school. While not perfect (its high class sizes would not be tolerated in a preferentially funded "faith" junior school) it has a good reputation for high standards and ethos. The head teacher, Mark Trott is open about his own Christian faith, and the school has good relationships with local churches and faith groups. The ethos of the school is strong, and displays much of what a faith school would call it's "Christian (or other) Values" Yet any local child can get a place at the school- which serves a range of highly affluent and also relatively poor areas of the town- exactly as it should be.

Rather than always assuming that the faith schools are best, it would do our leaders no harm to look at the great success of our best open and inclusive state schools!

Wednesday 23 April 2008
No other way

When teachers go on strike, it means there is no other way.

That, sadly is the position we have now reached. The last three years saw the value of our pay eroded by inflation. The imposed three year "settlement" of 2.45% followed by two years at 2.3% will have the same effect. That's six consecutive years of real-terms pay cuts.

Teachers living costs are increasing just like everybody else's. Council tax, food and utility bills have soared, and many teachers need to keep a watchful eye on their mortgage rates (that is, if they can get one. The average teacher can't get a mortgage on the average flat in nearly half of all towns !) The government claims that it needs to keep our wages down to combat inflation- but the evidence shows that teachers wages will have minimal effect, (this has been backed up by the Financial Times) The truth is that teachers are the victims of inflation, not the cause !

Teachers salaries start at nearly £3,000 less than comparable graduate jobs, and continue to fall behind during the first three years. Our young teachers have spent four years putting themselves through university- often with large student loans to pay off. (The Student Loans Company calculates it's "inflation based" interest rise at 4.8%... there's a surprise !) The government's own figures show that 50% of NQTs will leave the profession within 3 years.

This dispute comes as there are continuing signs that the government is making other major mistakes in education policy. Workload continues to grow- most of which is not related to the actual teaching of children ! The DCSF still has a bad case of initiative-itis, and schools minister Jim Knight told the ATL conference last month that he did not have a problem with classes of 70 children.

April 24th is a chance to send a clear message to government; teachers are highly skilled, highly valuable professionals, and should be paid fairly. Support your colleagues – support the profession !

Thanks to Bill Greenshields, my National President, and his local Derbyshire NUT division for the cartoon of the camel with the "last straw"- used during the pay ballot.

Thursday 24 April 2008
The day the teachers came out...

It is never a pleasure taking action against a Labour government, but sometimes there is no other way. That is why I was proud to be amongst hundreds of East Sussex teachers (and tens of thousands nationwide) who took part in the first national teachers strike for 22 years.

We had no way of knowing how well supported the action would be. The NUT has never "instructed" or compelled its members to join a strike- members have to weigh up the case for themselves. As the turnout was relatively low in our ballot (although considerably better that the turnout in most local elections) would other members join in?

Indeed, Labour minister Jim Knight kept mentioning the low ballot turnout, missing the point that only 28.5% of eligible adults voted for him in his Dorset constituency. If he wants to count not voting as being against the strike, then surely 71.5% of his constituents were "against" his election as MP ?[4]

As usual, sheer numbers did the talking. In Eastbourne every secondary school was affected- with Causeway shut completely, Bishop Bell running for just year 11, and my own school, Ratton, operating for years 9 and 11 only (in a school where another union, the NASUWT is bigger) Bourne, West Rise Infants, Highfield, Stone Cross and Hawkes Farm, were amongst the Primary schools closed completely, with most others partially affected.

Around 170 teachers came to a rally in the Cavendish Hotel, at which I joined local secretary Phil Clarke and speakers from other unions. It was also a pleasure to see Gill Roles, former Labour candidate for Eastbourne (2001) joining our demonstration, and doing some excellent work with the media.

I hope that the government will listen. I hope that they realise that public sector workers are the victims of inflation, NOT the cause. I hope they see that a three-year pay cut on top of a previous three year pay cut is not palatable (don't kid yourself that a below-inflation award is anything other than a pay cut !) If you want good teachers, you need to pay for them.

Above all, Gordon Brown needs to remember that teachers were the second most likely group of workers to vote Labour in 1997. We need to be building support where our strengths lie- not alienating our own voters!

Saturday 19 July 2008
Privatisation comes to Hastings

The academy programme has had a good deal of knocking in this blog, but, up until now, always in somebody else's patch. All that has now changed, with the recent announcement from East Sussex County Council, that it intends to **close down Hastings' three mixed secondary schools**, and replace them with two privatised academies.

The three schools, The Grove, Hillcrest and Filsham Valley, are currently part of an innovative project to turn them around. The head of Ninestiles school in Birmingham (turned around spectacularly, resulting in the knighthood…) Sir Dexter Hutt has a three year contract to run the schools as Executive Head, and to implement learning and behaviour systems to ensure a change in their fortunes.

Many people- including the NUT- were **cautiously supportive of this plan**, as it have us a mechanism to bring about school improvement and secure funding without having to go down the closure and privatisation route of the governments failing obsession of Academies.

Then, the **bombshell** came. At a mass meeting of teachers, parents, governors and union reps, Matt Dunkley, the county's Director of Children's Services announced that academy status was the **County's preferred route**, and that a plan had already been secretly drawn up for the schools to be closed (just as Sir Dexter's management moves into the "pursuit of excellence" phase !) and for their management and governance to be taken over by a consortium headed by the **University of Brighton** (the main sponsor: universities don't have to **cough up the £2m** fee !) with **British Telecom** as their partner (my fluctuating broadband connection does not fill me with confidence in this company) and East Sussex County Council remaining a **minor** partner. This option is being touted as the "best" (or at least the "least worse") structure for an academy project: rather like trying to sell the **"best" kind of typhoid**...

East Sussex (Tory) fiercely resisted the attempts to break up local authorities via schools opting out as Grant Maintained schools, in the mid-1990's. My current school, Ratton, tried to go down this route: thanks to a campaign by parents, the County, staff and trade unions, the proposals were rejected in a parental ballot by 85%. Why have the East Sussex Tories so spectacularly changed their minds?

There is clearly going to be a fight over this. Already, despite protestations of the pro-union credentials of the new consortium, my local officers have already been **barred** from entering two of the schools and speaking to members (so much for consultation: and the academy is still up to three years away !) All of the trade unions, including the traditionally non-combatant ATL are firmly and fiercely opposed to privatisation. **Watch this space for more**.

The Academies project is the brainchild of **"Lord" Andrew Adonis**: a former Labour policy adviser who has never taught a class in his life. Adonis has never been elected- or at least not as Labour: he was a **Lib Dem** councillor for some years, and adopted to be a Lib Dem parliamentary candidate, although never stood. He defected to Labour around the time of the 1997 victory (funny that) although never deigned to lower himself to seeking selection for a democratically accountable Labour seat- preferring the job for life that membership of the House of Lords brings. This also leaves him in the clear to **defect straight to the Tories** in the event that "Call me Dave" Cameron gets in- the Tories have already issued an open invitation to him ![5]

Is it any wonder that this carpetbagger -**who makes me ashamed to share a party with him**- wants to end any democratic (or indeed parental) accountability for our schools.

The privately-educated Adonis has clearly swallowed all of the guff that his housemaster would have told him about the dreadful working class, pierced, tattooed, gun wielding, baby-eating pupils in the state sector. Hence, his pronouncements that the way to turn round "failing" schools is to access the **"educational DNA"** of the private schools. My General Secretary (acting) **Christine Blowers**, put it much better: "we don't want their DNA- we just want their funding"

Give any school the facilities, the class size and the freedom from bureaucracy and DCSF diktats, and we'll show you who has the real "Educational DNA"

Saturday 19 July 2008
Hastings Academy: Madness !

*Following the earlier post about **academies**: a copy of a general news release that was distributed at, and following, the official announcement of the closure of the Hastings schools. It appears here in full[6]:*

The NUT has been **cautiously supportive** of the forthcoming three-year federation of The Grove, Hillcrest and Filsham Valley, under the leadership of Sir Dexter Hutt and the **Ninestiles** team. We were led to believe that this course of action would give additional resources and support to the schools, in order to help them raise standards, and continue to exist as three comprehensive community schools, serving their local area.

How wrong we were !

East Sussex recently announced that the preferred plan is to let the Ninestiles team lead improvement in the three schools… get standards up… and then…

CLOSE all three schools down, and replace them with two privatised Academy schools.

In other words, after three years, they want to start all over again ! This is a **slap in the face** to teachers, parents and the local community from our own elected representatives.

The **NUT** (and the other TUC-affiliated teachers associations) remains firmly opposed to the **privatisation** of our schools through the Academy programme. We believe that every child has the right to attend a good local school, and that schools should be accountable to parents and the communities they serve.

Visit the Anti-Academies Alliance at or Campaign for State Education websites, or read Francis Beckett's excellent book *"The Great City Academy Fraud"* to find out more about why privatising schools is not the answer !

In the meantime, contact your local **County Councillor** and ask them why they have decided to condemn The Grove, Hillcrest and Filsham Valley before the federation's work has even started?

ALL DIFFERENT, ALL EQUAL

If the Labour Party (or the left in general) is not a crusade for fairness and equality, then it is nothing. And for many years, especially given the policies of the last Tory government, homophobia was seen as the last socially-accepted prejudice by many. Thankfully, the end of Section 28, the end of the ban on LGBT in the military, the equality at work regulations and the recognition of Civil Partnerships have made a real difference, and even the Tory front bench now supports these measures. Not some unreconstructed Tory right-wingers, however. One of them is, at the time of writing, my local MP.

Friday, 15 June 2007
Most homophobic MP in Westminster ?

I was chuffed that the Eastbourne Herald ran a story I gave them today, regarding the Tory MP for Eastbourne, stating[1]:

"EASTBOURNE MP Nigel Waterson has been described as the 'most homophobic MP in Westminster' by a local Labour spokesman.

Dave Brinson, the chair of Eastbourne Labour Party, backed claims by deputy leadership contender Hazel Blears that the Conservative Party is 'riddled with homophobia', citing the voting record of Mr Waterson.In the week when the Tory party defended itself against Ms Blears' claims, Mr Brinson questioned why the Eastbourne MP retains his front bench job, despite 'disagreeing with his leader over equality laws'.

"Nigel Waterson has been an opponent of every piece of legislation that has sought to promote equality for gay and lesbian citizens," said Mr Brinson."Indeed, he spoke strongly in the Commons against the repeal of the bully's charter Section 28. The Tory chairman Francis Maude has apologised for voting for Section 28 in 1988, and even Michael Howard has admitted that he was wrong.

"David Cameron supports civil partnerships, and has made serious, if not necessarily credible, attempts to woo the gay and lesbian vote.

"While there are always disagreements over policy in any party, the tradition is that those who can't agree with the leadership should not serve on the front bench — as proved during the recent grammar schools row."Why on earth is Nigel Waterson, who is so obviously at odds with Cameron on important equality issues, allowed to keep his job?"

However, Mr Waterson hit back by saying he was 'certainly not going to be drawn into the Labour Party deputy leadership contest, as the candidates seem to be vying for who can be the most absurdly extreme and left wing'. Strangely he gave no indication whether or not he agreed with the sentiments of his current or previous party leader….

Saturday, 16 June 2007
More on "homophobic" Waterson

I have had good responses from local friends over yesterday's Eastbourne Herald article (see previous post) It is also interesting to look at the responses published on the Herald website.

One is a typical "outraged of Tunbridge Wells" style response, calling homosexuality an unnatural practice, and attacking gay pride and other things that "push homosexuality" at him. There is a good response against this, though.

The other interested me more- that was from "Jo" who posted the following:

"As a proud mum of a Lesbian daughter I felt I have some right to reply to this article. I am really sick to death of the posturing by Labour over any issue they think can give them a 'Political Advantage'. Nigel is quite right this was a free vote. I suspect Labour and the LibDems got together over this issue. I have met Nigel, I told him how many children I have, and that one of them was 'Gay', his reply? "I should hope you do not love her any less than the others" - Is that Homophobic? I don't think so. This 'story' is a sorry attempt at 'Political' points gaining, and does not impress someone who comes from a long line of Labour supporters.[2]"

This raises a few interesting points for discussion. If this is the Jo of Sovereign Harbour that I think it is (and may be wrong) she is indeed from a family of Labour supporters, but is also a very pleasant, down to earth Tory activist; which explains her angle on this story !

1. Is it wrong for political parties to promote the success of policies proposed and enacted by their MP's against opposition from other parties ? Is that not democratic politics ?

2. Some issues are traditionally on a "free vote" (abortion, etc.) However, if David Cameron is regularly talking up civil partnerships, equalities and the number of LGB candidates in his speeches and interviews, is it not appropriate that his MP's record is open to scrutiny ?

3. I don't doubt the sincerity of Nigel's "love" question, but that is not the point here; it is about whether he supports Jo's daughter's right to have her partnership recognised, to not be discriminated against at work or in the marketplace, etc. Nigel's record on these is atrocious.

4. Pre-Cameron, Nigel Waterson's leaflets regularly featured nasty little comments about gay rights and section 28. So yes, that IS homophobic.

5. No, we didn't get together with the Lib Dems- we don't get on very well with them in Eastbourne !

It is interesting how prickly Waterson and the local Tory faithful are on this issue. Cameron is certainly trying to shed the old homophobic, prejudiced "nasty party" image, but he is going to need a clear out of right wing MPs and local activists first.

Equality issues may not be high on the list of traditional election subjects, but for LGBT people and their families, the thought of casting a vote for an MP who disagrees with their lifestyle and opposes every piece of progress towards equality, it could be a problem for Waterson in a town with a thriving LGBT community and a Tory majority of only 1,124 (not, sadly, over us !)

Sunday 17 June 2007
I am not a Lib Dem !

Last comment on the "homophobic Tory" story... I was going to move on, but the Herald comments page has a reply from "Jo" that made me giggle quite a lot. It is reproduced in full here:-

"Dave- I don't know as Mr Cameron has used the Gay Rights as a campaign issue, I know he has stated his beliefs which is another thing, it is still a free vote issue. I am not really interested in what 'your party' believes in. I used to have quite a healthy respect for any politician who stuck firmly to their beliefs. It is not so long ago that one of yours could not even have the guts to admit to his homosexuality (maybe that was because of the dirty campaign he fought against Peter Tatchell some time back). But what really got me was when after espousing 'family values' and morality during a Commons debate yet another of your MP's got caught out in a 'Gay rent boy' scandal. Now it wasn't so much the hypocrisy of it, which was bad enough. But he has never ever taken full responsibility of his actions, as far as I know he still blames 'pressure through a rough time of leadership problems'. So please don't lecture me on such issues. I suggest you ask your 'political elite' to get their own acts together. [3]"

Valid point, you may think. However, the one glaring problem is that she seems a bit confused about my party affiliation- both the MP's mentioned are, in fact **Lib Dems**. Now you can call me most things.....

The bisexual MP who fought a dirty campaign against Peter Tatchell was Simon Hughes- a Lib Dem. Tatchell was the Labour candidate, and faced homophobia not just from Hughes' supporters, but John O'Grady an independent "Real Labour" candidate and former leader of Southwark Council. I strongly recommend reading Tatchell's book *The Battle for Bermondsey,* which shows how far we've come since Liberal canvassers went round wearing badges saying "I've been kissed by Peter Tatchell" and Simon Hughes put out a Focus leaflet describing himself as "The Straight Choice"[4].

I really don't like the direction that this story is going- we had enough of the sex lives of MPs during the 1990's after John Major's ill-fated "Back to Basics" family values campaign. But it is hypocritical of politicians (priests, commentators, captains of industry etc.) on any side to say one thing in campaigns or speeches and then do the opposite. No wonder the trust rating for our elected officials is so low!

Monday 6 August 2007
Labour and proud !

I was proud to march with the Labour Campaign for Lesbian and Gay Rights in the Brighton Pride parade on Saturday. The Pride movement has grown from being a purely "political" demonstration, to being a real festival celebrating diversity. The parade was followed by a huge gathering at Preston Park, with music, shopping, information stalls and a real party atmosphere- thousands of people, not just the LGBT community, but our friends, families, children, pets etc. joining for a day out to celebrate how far we've come.

The turnout was incredible, and we were joined in the parade (alongside the "commercial" floats from every bar in Brighton) by a range of political and community groups. Many trade unions took part (not the NUT this year- we'll have to get that sorted for 2008) and other political parties, including, unbelievably, the Brighton Tories.

The Tories are standing the gay-friendly Dr David Bull in the Pavilion constituency, and his little gang were handing out cards saying how pro-gay David Cameron's Tories are. Hopefully, most Brighton voters have longer memories than he does.

The Labour government repealed Section 28- that prevented education authorities from "promoting homosexuality as a pretended family relationship". In reality, this meant that teachers and schools were uneasy about discussing sexual orientation, and in many cases were not confident in robustly challenging homophobia and anti-gay bullying. The Tories defended Section 28 to the end- one of the main speakers against its repeal was Nigel Waterson MP.

The Labour government equalised the age of consent at 16- saying that our young people had stewardship over their own bodies at that age, regardless of their personal orientation. (The gay age of consent was 21 until 1995- when Parliament voted to lower it to 18. Nigel Waterson voted to keep it at 21.)

The Labour Government ended the ban on gay and lesbian people serving in the Armed Forces. Under the Tories, service people were investigated and dishonourably discharged (ie. sacked) from the forces simply for being gay. The Labour Government introduced the Civil Partnership- allowing lesbian and gay couples to recognise their partnership in law (marriage by any other name.) Nigel Waterson and the majority of Tories voted against this. In a survey of 1,294 Conservative Party activists, a THIRD of said that they would NOT be willing to attend the Civil Partnership ceremony of a friend[5].

The Equality Act, introduced by the Labour Government made it illegal for people to be discriminated against in employment or in the provision of goods and services because of the sexual orientation. Under the Tories, it was perfectly legal to sack somebody just for being gay.

For all the warm words of Tories in selective areas (like Brighton with a well organised Gay and Lesbian population) they still keep confirmed homophobes like Nigel Waterson, who has voted against every piece of equality legislation, on their front bench.

THE AIRBOURNE FIASCO

Airbourne has, for many years, been one of the highlights of the summer in Eastbourne- a town which still relies heavily on tourism for our local economy. In 2008, the council, in its wisdom, proposed to end Airbourne as a free event, and charge the public to enter the key areas of the seafront. Very few did !

These columns chart the rise of the campaign to keep Airbourne free, and also look at previous clangers by the "experts" responsible for tourism in this town.

Saturday, 14 June 2008
The original *Airbourne* rip-off

A story about me, Airbourne, and some "magic" deckchairs...

I used to work on Eastbourne deckchairs. As a student (and then as a what-shall-I-do-with-life graduate) I spent six glorious summers enjoying the sun and sea air, (and earning a few pence over the Minimum Wage…) *Airbourne* was always a busy time for us: we knew that every chair that was put out would be taken- sometimes several times- and our takings would be huge (for the years when we got commission, this was a good thing!)

In 2001, the **invisible middle-management** (we were lucky to see them a couple of times a season) came up with a jolly wheeze to screw the public during the "free" airshow: **£5 deckchair** tickets.

Basically, we were to take the 300 newest chairs off the busy eastern promenade, and put them on a "special" beach near the Wish Tower slopes. Members of the public would obviously flock to sit on a beach that was different from, well, any other beach, and pay five times the going rate for sitting in a "special" chair.

To the out-of-touch brains (then based safely away from the actual seafront) this seemed an excellent idea. To those of us who knew the customers, **it was a rip off**. And the public ended up agreeing. Less than 100 "special" chairs were sold over the weekend: mainly because there were no chairs available elsewhere at the normal rate. The grand scheme therefore made the council under £500- less the cost of employing an extra member of staff to man the "special" beach. Had the chairs been left to do what they did for the rest of the season, every single one would have been hired, more than doubling the revenue, without alienating regular customers or leaving tourists with a lasting impression of **rip-off Eastbourne**.

What really opened my eyes was the spin, **half-truth and utter rubbish that was spewed out by the council in order to try and justify this scheme.**

- **There were 2,000 chairs available:** This figure counted the bandstand seats, which, surprisingly, were only available during the band concerts, *(speaks slowly)* what with it being a bandstand... see? It would have been just as "honest" to also count the seats in the Congress Theatre, the Redoubt and the Wish Tower café…

- **They were brand new chairs, not taken out of service**: The first bit was true, the second bit was from a manager who either did not know what was going on in his own department, or was a bare-faced liar. Paying bottoms had been in the "special" chairs for more than ten weeks before- up on the normal promenades at the normal price.
- **The £5 gave prestige position on a private beach**: Well, as the attendant found out, it is not possible to keep the public off Eastbourne beach. Various tourists pointed out that the beach was not "closed" (because we were letting people on, albeit for a fiver), that no bye-law or order gave the council the power to do it, and most of the beach was below the high water mark, which meant that it was none of the council's business.

In the end, I allowed the *Herald* journalist (who had been having a field day with this story that just ran on and on !) to name me as the source of his information about the numbers sold: mainly to protect other staff in the department, who were worried that they would be blamed instead.

I was carpeted by the manager in one of his rare visits, although **he declined an offer to formally discipline me, with union representation**. Instead, I was told not to ask for a reference, as he could not comment favourably on **my** trustworthiness (ironic, given the misinformation he was happy to feed to the trusting council tax payers of Eastbourne!) I continued to work until the end of the season, and then went off to do my teacher-training.

The following year, I got a job teaching in one of the language schools: although did put in an application for the deckchairs, at half the wages, just to see what happened. Predictably, I was **not even given the courtesy of a rejection**. Six years later - last summer in fact- I heard that they were recruiting for evening bandstand staff. The response of the management was reported to me as "no way!" Nice to know that some people have got nothing better to do than bear a grudge...

So now, we are to lose the **best free airshow in the country**. Residents and tourists alike will have to fork out a fiver (again) or, more likely, just watch the Red Arrows from the downs, Beachy Head etc. and forgo the rest of the demonstrations, stalls etc. Numbers will plummet, exhibitors, stallholders and sponsors will notice the rapidly diminishing number of customers, and a slippery slope will ensue. The Lib Dem council will make a **short term cash gain, for a long term huge loss.** (for once, Tory columnist Ian Lucas and I are in agreement. Let's not make a habit of that...) [2]

Sunday 7 September 2008
Airbourne: We told you so !

I used to enjoy Airbourne. For my student years I worked on Eastbourne's seafront deckchair operation, and got to see the whole show while being paid! This year, of course, that situation was reversed. (I got **blackballed** by the tourism department of EBC because I whistleblew about their absurd £5 deckchair scam in 2001- as detailed in my article of 14th June this year.)

In the *Eastbourne Herald* that week, I warned that the harebrained Lib Dem scheme to charge admission for this year's show would be a disaster[3].

And how ! The first day of the festival saw great coverage on local TV news. The cameras gleefully filmed the empty East promenades, that in previous years were standing room only.
The council admitted that this year's festival has lost **£360,000.** This includes:

- **£100,000** bill from the **police** *(they will police free events for nothing but, quite rightly, charge for a commercial event. None of the highly paid events staff knew this rather basic piece of event organisation information.)*
- c**£40,000** for the **security fences** to keep the great unwashed off their own seafront.
- c**£60,000** for the **ticketing** arrangements (an outside contractor)

....indeed, the Eastbourne Herald quotes a figure of **£250,000** on top of the costs that would usually have been incurred by the free festival. Nobody knows whether any **legal action** is being pursued by the stallholders who were charged upwards of £1000 for their pitches, expecting the six figure attendances of previous years, only to get the pitiful throng of less than 50,000 this year.

My only visit to Airbourne this year was to support Shirley Moth and her gang from the ***I'm Not Paying to Stand on my Own Seafront*** group. This is a fiercely politically independent group, although Nigel Waterson MP expressed his support for the group at an earlier demonstration, along with several other councillors from the opposition group. The Lib Dem activists were clearly told to keep their heads down *(not even **Stephen Lloyd** had the front to put in an appearance, and that isn't a phrase you can use often !)* but I know that a lot of ordinary Lib Dem supporters also fully endorsed the campaign against Airbourne charges.

On the first day, the group convened on the first free beach East of the pier, and then, at low-tide walked with the banner across the groynes at the low water mark into the restricted area: where there were no fences or stewards as the Council has no jurisdiction beyond this point. The banner was proudly planted on the beach to cheers and applause from customers on the pier- which proved to be the best free viewing spot.

The council had expected a **£192,000 profit** from ticket sales of **£450,000** (The correct teenage response is "Yeah, right.") The real figure was almost £300,000 below this. **So what to do about Airbourne ?** Even with a significant sponsorship drive, it looks likely that the council will have to subsidise the show. **I'm not against that.**

A **sensible** level of subsidy would be appropriate in any town with an economy that features tourism as a significant player. This should be **clearly budgeted and made known to the council tax payers well in advance**- not as the "loss" but as the "cost" of staging this important (free) event. The officers and the councillors will have to get round the table together, to see if a realistic package can be put together to save this show for future years.

Eastbourne will regret it if we don't !

Sunday 7 September 2008
Where are our "Leaders" ?

The following letter from me was published in the Eastbourne Herald on Friday 5th September:

"Am I the only person feeling a bit sorry for **Norman Kinnish**?

Norman is a paid senior official of the borough council, whose job it is to implement decisions made by the elected councillors. He is an employee, not a councillor. Yet during the Airbourne fiasco, he seemed to be **wheeled out** at every opportunity, whether in the papers or on TV, to defend a decision made by the politicians.

Meanwhile, **David Tutt**, the supposed leader of the council kept his head well down, finally surfacing last week to promise a thorough enquiry into… well… his own decision. My former comrade Steve Wallis, officially the elected member responsible for tourism, continues to demonstrate an invisibility of which Macavity would have been proud.

Certainly the elected councillors were poorly advised – not least over the fiasco of the "surprise" police bill. But they should stop trying to blame the staff, and recognise that having agreed to implement the charges, they should have the **integrity to accept responsibility** for their decisions.

Dave Brinson, Labour Parliamentary Candidate for Eastbourne, South Street, Eastbourne." [4]

In their defence, the same edition of the Herald carries an article entitled "I put my hands up to the failure" where David Tutt apologises[5]. *Norman Kinnish is quoted in the article as "refusing to point the finger of blame." Tutt, on the other hand manages to point the finger of blame quite squarely at the officers. There's leadership for you !*

UP THE WORKERS

The 20th Century (and to an extent, the latter part of the 19th) saw the growth of the concept of the working man or woman having rights and dignity as a person, not just as a commodity of the bosses. As a lifelong trade unionist, I am proud of the role that workers' organisations- the Trade Unions- have played in every single piece of protection for working people, whether a living wage, holidays and maternity rights, or simple health and safety legislation that means it is not acceptable to place working people at undue risk. A few issues during the life of the column stirred my trade unionist principles- here are some of them.

Wednesday 15 August 2007
Solidarność !

On my way to the bar after a Labour Party meeting in Eastbourne last week, I was stopped by a young guy, and asked why we weren't holding our meeting at the "Polish Club." Warming to his theme, he tried again as I was leaving, to enquire "how much Polish I spoke…"

I confess that, being quite late, and after a fairly animated local party meeting, I exchanged pleasantries and avoided the political dimension of his question. But it is an interesting theme to explore, especially as it is likely to come up in the General Election.

Eastbourne has a very low minority-ethnic population, notwithstanding a number of East European workers coming into the town. Yet race has often been an issue in past elections. At the start of this decade, the local Conservatives frequently used asylum seekers as a topic in local newsletters. More worryingly still, the National Front were active in the town in the 1970's (and stood as recently as the 1990 by-election) and briefly, a few years ago, the fascist BNP claimed it had an "Organiser" in the town- although thankfully very little evidence of him actually organising!

Attitudes have pleasantly changed. This year, right-wing local MP Nigel Waterson has praised Eastbourne as a "richly diverse place" and paid warm tribute both to the Polish community in the town, and to the residents of Bangladeshi origins[1]. Yet, there is already some disquiet being aired, especially by young unemployed or low-wage employees about East European migration.

Migration has never been a root cause of unemployment in this country. Large scale immigration in the 1950's was due to a labour shortage- with many migrant workers coming to Britain to fill low wage jobs. The NHS would not have survived the 1990's had it not been for the willingness of overseas-born and trained staff to relocate to Britain to fill vacancies. And, in the main, the migration from Easter Europe has been filling jobs where there were significant vacancies – often requiring workers with specific, shortage, skills.

As a socialist, I have to ask two questions to evaluate the fairness of the employment of migrant workers:
1. Are they being employed to fill vacancies that other workers did not apply for, were not qualified to do, or not most suitable for?

2. Are they being exploited by firms who are using them to undercut other workers, to subvert employment rights or to avoid minimum wage regulations?

If the answer is (1) then there should be very little problem. Under our membership of the EU, workers can move freely between member states (as more than a million Britons have done) to work and live. If British-born workers are not available with suitable qualifications then it is only to the good of the economy that we can recruit from elsewhere. **However, the government needs to act swiftly if there is evidence of the second.**

In Derby last week, 15 young Hungarian workers were dismissed from their jobs at Domino's Pizza. They were paid less than British counterparts, put up in accommodation tied to their job, and being forced into a spiral of debt by unfair (if not unlawful) deductions from their wages. When they joined the *Unite-T&G* union to fight their corner, they were sacked- in gross defiance of British employment law[2].

The Labour government has, rightly identified that appropriate migration is a benefit both to the nation's economy and to the workers coming to offer their labour to Britain. But in order to safeguard these new workers from exploitation, and to avoid a perception from British-born workers that they are "taking our jobs" there are a number of steps that need to be taken:

- Ensure that all migrant workers are fully informed about British law regarding Minimum Wage, working time, compulsory holiday pay etc. and provide the resources for the prosecution and significant punishment of employers who break the law.
- Tighten up equalities law to deal with companies that are clearly offering a lower rate of pay to migrant workers for doing the same job as British counterparts. As well as ending exploitation, this would also reassure British-born workers that they are not losing out because they are being undercut in wages.
- Encourage the recruitment of migrant workers into our trade unions, who negotiate appropriate and fair wages and conditions in the workplace- for all staff irrespective of background.
- If we succeed, then we can continue building a strong economy with supportive and cohesive communities. If not, then we risk the ugly face of racism rearing its head once more.

Thursday 30 August 2007
The porridge hots up !

Turning on the radio on Wednesday, I was a little surprised not to be able to enjoy Showaddywaddy, the Sweet and the Jam pumping out. ITV schedules were conspicuously devoid of Emergency Ward 10, World of Sport wrestling and Mike Yarwood. My ties had not morphed into the kipper style. And yet, according to a brace of right wing commentators, the 1970's were back.

I refer, of course to the industrial action by the Prison Officers' Association. A "wildcat" strike, apparently advertised to shop stewards only an hour before the pickets were out, and without the union politely giving the employer the statutory week's notice. The Tories were cock-a-hoop, Labour politicians roundly condemned the action and the Home Office (sorry…Ministry of Justice…) hot-footed it to the High Court for an injunction.

Yes, the strike was wrong. As the rest of us in the trade union movement patiently go along, to the letter, with the legal niceties before taking action (which, incidentally, we do as a last resort) and, in the meantime promote positive, constructive, moderate-but-forthright unionism, it only takes one piece of action like this to undo all of the good work.

However, this is not the 1970's. There is no closed shop. Trade unions have little power to discipline their members who cross picket lines, and even if they did, those members could and would simply leave the union. What has happened to make prison officers so angry in every single public sector prison in the land, that they will down tools in an unofficial strike with an hour's notice?

Labour ministers need to take notice. So many of the new generation of advisers and policy experts have worked in that field all of their careers, and don't always judge the mood of ordinary people in ordinary jobs. Strike action is a hardship for those taking it- how many of them can really afford to lose a day's wages ? But action like yesterday's is a clear symptom that they have been pushed to the limit, and we hadn't noticed!

Gordon Brown (formerly the "Iron Chancellor") has already announced a "guideline" of 2% for wage increases in the public sector. Already, though, pragmatism has led to an improved offer for frontline NHS workers. The problem with 2% is that, with inflation running at twice that in real terms, it is, in fact a wage cut. To workers in the public sector, many of whom are on wages much lower than the national average, it means their bills, their household expenses, their fares etc. will be increasing at twice the rate of their pay packet. As an economic policy, no doubt 2% is foolproof. As a real world policy dealing with real people, it is highly inflammatory!

How does Gordon keep his inflation target on track without cutting the real value of millions of pay packets among workers who are statistically more likely to vote Labour? First, we need to see salaries as an investment in the public sector, just as valuable as extending hours and building programmes. Diminishing wages in key services will drive more and more talented people into jumping ship for more lucrative roles in the private sector.

Secondly, an old fashioned idea. Trade unions often used to submit a wage claim that was based on X % or a flat rate increase of £Y per week, whichever was the greater. This- call it Old-Labour redistribution if you like- meant that the staff on the lowest grades received a more meaningful increase. As a teacher (so facing the 2% squeeze with the rest!) I would be more inclined to accept restraint in my salary rise if it meant that the teaching assistants I work alongside with every day were going to get a decent increase to their, often quite insultingly low, take home pay.

In 1997, a breakdown of the groups who voted Labour showed nurses and teachers as among the most solid supporters. A Labour Government that loses the faith of these hard working public servants does so at its electoral peril.

Tuesday, 29 January 2008
Is the carthorse sleeping ?

There is a local association of my union who have recently got a bee in their bonnet about the Trades Union Congress- the umbrella organisation to which virtually all of Britain's unions belong. At Annual Conference they submit a motion for the NUT to withdraw from the TUC- and every year it fails to make it onto the agenda. They then have the cunning idea of trying to work it into an amendment to a motion, on anything from school funding to supporting trainee teachers.

Let's imagine (as may well happen) a motion is put to the conference congratulating Jamie Oliver on his work in campaigning to raise the quality of school dinners. This organisation would table an amendment along the lines of:

"Conference further notes that, despite Mr Oliver's worthy campaign, the TUC has never congratulated him on his campaign. Conference believes that this is an absolute disgrace, and therefore resolves to withdraw from the TUC immediately...."

Fortunately, you can usually count on one hand the number of delegates who will support them, as virtually every trade union member recognises the good work that the TUC does, in terms of lobbying, research, mediation and general communication between member unions.

However, in the latest round of pay deals, I begin to wonder quite what the TUC has been up to (or not, as the case may be…) Has the old carthorse been caught in an extended nap?

The government's 2% target for public sector pay is plain wrong. Inflation is caused by a number of factors- the money supply, exports, growth as well as wages. It certainly is not caused solely by public sector wages- yet that is the implication as wage rises in the private sector are getting much closer to a 4% average- in line with the Retail Price Index (instead of the selective CPI) that government used to use to measure inflation (and still does when it is calculating the interest on student loans….) Inflation is 4%. Deal with it!

The unions could have made a coherent, popular case against the 2% target (and I don't mean a "winter of discontent"; a united response would have brought the government to negotiation without a single day lost to strikes.)

However, in the NHS negotiations, Unison accepted a deal. In the local government round, Unite and GMB accepted a deal- Unison balloted for a strike, but then got lukewarm on whether it was urging its members to vote for or against, and in the end got a very indecisive result.

Following last week's teachers' deal, my union the NUT has announced a ballot, as we have always maintained we would if the offer did not keep up with inflation (4%- as I'm going to keep pointing out !) It is, however a difficult position to be in now, as many lower paid workers have accepted deals less generous than ours. Rival teachers union NASUWT praised the deal (although their General Secretary got slightly cold feet shortly afterwards, and has shut up while her union "polls" its members for opinion.) The other education union ATL (mainly private and grammar schools) welcomes the pay award, but couldn't really do much else, being the most painfully non-confrontational union imaginable.

The Prison Officers are still spoiling for a fight after their impromptu walk out in the summer, and the frontline civil servants of PCS- amongst the lowest paid in the public sector- remain united, militant, and balloting for more strike action.

All of these unions are in the TUC- and yet all the messages are different. Not so much a chorus from the organised workforce as a grating cacophony; which means that the treasury hacks, policy wonks, economists and assorted right-wing commentators go without facing a coherent and structured challenge on behalf of working people- who are the ones who will suffer.

Of course, the TUC has other concerns than private sector pay- it has a majority of its member unions organising in the private sector after all. It cannot necessarily "speak" on behalf of all the disparate member organisations. But what it can do is bang a few heads together, and point out that if we approach this threat to our members living standards divided, then the outcome is inevitable failure. If we can speak with one voice, then surely a solution can be found. Isn't that why we are trade unionists in the first place?

Tuesday, 10 June 2008
Primark exploits Eastbourne youngsters

I was walking through the local Arndale Centre, when I saw that discount clothing store **Primark** was advertising for staff. How well does this fantastically successful national company reward its, mainly young, staff I wondered...

The advert in its window advertised vacancies at:

- **£5.69** for staff 22 and over. compared to...
- **£5.07** per hour for staff aged 18-21, and a mere..
- **£3.80** for those 16 and 17 !

Obviously, in Primark-land, your labouring is only worth the borderline poverty-pay minimum wage once you have reached your 22nd birthday. Until then, they take advantage of a loophole in the law, that renders you **worth less than the lowest paid 22 year-old in the country.**
Primark are increasingly rare in the retail sector. Many big companies have moved away from discriminatory pay policies: for instance **ASDA** scrapped all age-related rates back in 2006[3].

Indeed, Primark only seem to consider its young workers as **lower-than-low** in England. They abolished their junior rates of pay for workers in Northern Ireland (part of the UK the last time I checked) in 2006- why is a Belfast teenager any more a full, adult citizen than an Eastbourne one ?

The National Minimum Wage is one of the proudest achievements of the Labour Government. **The Tories opposed it tooth and nail**- John Major said that the very idea of a minimum wage was immoral. He was backed up by leading **Lib Dems** including Ming Campbell.

I remember when the minimum wage came in. I had been doing part time and student jobs, and pocketing only **£3 per hour**, until Tony Blair raised that to £3.60 for me. That has steadily risen, above inflation rates, to today's **£5.52**

When Labour brought in the minimum wage, there was a lower rate for 18-21 year olds. This was envisaged as a **short term measure**, while the economy adapted to having a minimum wage law. At the time, I was proud to support the **GMB** Union's Rage Against Age Rates ("ROAR") campaign to end the lower rate.

Nearly ten years on, it is time to end this piece of state-sanctioned age discrimination against our young people.

If you are considered to be an **adult at 18** in every other area of the law- including voting and standing for Parliament- surely you should receive the same protection against Scrooge-like employers?

Thursday, 23 October 2008
Support working parents, Peter

The government has announced that it is to **review** plans to increase the right for parents to request **flexible working patterns**, because of the economic situation.

A spokesperson for **Peter Mandelson's** Business Department said:

"We are looking at the appropriateness of new regulations that are due to come into force - that includes employment regulations. We can confirm that no decisions to halt regulations have been made"[5]

Brendan Barber, General Secretary of the **Trades Union Congress** hit back, however, calling the announcement *"irrelevant"* to the current economic situation, and warning that the government could *"send a message to working parents that the government is not on their side"*

The government was right to propose these rights: they must stand firm.

At the moment, parents with children under 5 have a right to **request** a change in their working pattern. The employer must give this proper consideration, and, if they are unable to grant the request, they must **explain their reasons for doing so**. This would, of course cover legitimate pressures to a business in the current economic climate. The new proposals extend that right to parents with children under 16.

The Labour Party **backed the proposals at our conference** in the autumn, and they were based on an independent inquiry headed by Imelda Walsh, human resources director at *Sainsbury's*.

Like most employment legislation, it is necessary only for some firms, as many **good organisations already have policies that recognise the importance of the (many different types of) family, and the pressures of parenthood**. Those firms would be unaffected. It is only where employers will not even entertain the idea who will be compelled into considering such requests, and justifying their reasons if they can't accede.

Sarah Jackson, the chief executive of Working Families, a pressure group, said:
"Scrapping flexible working hours would actively prevent people from getting access to something that could really help their businesses.

Mandelson should be making every effort to give business people the tools they need in a downturn ... When people are worried about their jobs, you need to find every way possible to give them a morale boost and get them working better for you."[6]

To reduce hours is a difficult decision for any working parent: often balancing a loss of income against their caring responsibilities. When a parent or carer wishes to make such an adjustment, surely it is reasonable to expect their employer to consider that seriously and respectfully. That isn't burdensome red tape, it is the least we would expect in a **civilized society**.

The government needs to stand firm.

LAW AND LIBERTY

Issues of law, human rights and personal freedom do not always make for the sexiest, most exciting columns, but they are at the heart of any free country. On several occasions during the life of this column, I have been moved to muse on issues of religious freedom, civil liberties, and, right at the end of the column's life- that of assisted dying and euthanasia.

Since the columns have been published, the issue of the right to die has taken a higher media position- not least with the acclaimed lecture from Alzheimer's sufferer Sir Terry Pratchett. If and when I start writing the column again, this issue is bound to come up again- and I look forward to taking part in that debate.

Sunday 17 February 2008
Leave my Bishop alone

I have never been a fan of the "established" part of the Church of England (the constitutional link between church and state). I don't like the fact that Margaret Thatcher (a Methodist) got to decide who were appointed bishops in the Church of England. I don't like the fact that the decision of our synod to ordain women priest had to get the approval of the House of Commons, and MP's such as Nigel Waterson (a Roman Catholic) could vote to overturn the decision of the church members. So, I am not keen on the recent free-for-all over Archbishop Rowan Williams' (ill-thought out) comments about Sharia Law.

The Sun took the opportunity to get in several "witty" headlines, ranging from WHAT A BURKHA to the slightly smutty BASH THE BISHOP, and encouraged readers to return cut-out coupons to call for Dr Williams' resignation. I would imagine that the majority of those who did have not attended many Sunday services at Anglican churches recently. So why is the leader of just one of the many religious groups in our country considered fair game for disinterested parties to attack?

For the record (and as a practicing and active Anglican, please note !) I don't agree with the sentiments of what the Archbishop said. He didn't call for Sharia Law to be given parallel status with UK law, he did, to some extent, acknowledge what is already happening. Ten unofficial Sharia courts already exist in Britain, and advise or arbitrate for devout Muslims on issues such as divorce, financial matters and how to live a devout lifestyle. They have no legal status, and are not dissimilar in some ways to a Christian seeking advice and confession with their minister- albeit rather more formal!

This use of informal Sharia Law is going to continue, and if participants are willing (I have concerns about the status of women in some family related matters) is not a matter for anyone else. The danger is that this will escalate demands from more radical groups for Sharia to be more widely introduced, and formally recognised under UK law, and that, I think, is what many interpreted the Archbishop as condoning, which I don't believe he did!

The most literal and fundamentalist applications of Sharia specify draconian punishments such as death for apostasy (deserting the Islamic faith) and adultery, amputation for theft and flogging for drunkenness.

Of course, the vast majority of Islamic countries, while retaining elements of

Sharia Law, do not implement this level of punishment (although gay men still face the death penalty in Iran, and in our "ally" Saudi Arabia) But it is the reporting of this extreme interpretation of Sharia Law that sells newspapers. Cartoonist Martin Rowson considers that the Archbishop "threw himself into the lion's den... by using the trigger words 'Sharia Law'"

Roswson goes on to eloquently speculate on what the Archbishop meant to convey, and it's worth considering:

"Williams is a thoughtful and complex man, whose liberal credentials are impeccable. You can, therefore, interpret his exasperatingly opaque comments as an entirely commendable plea for parity under the law, to protect and empower poor, powerless Muslims living in Britain, and counter the deprivation, racism and substitute racism many of them endure. After all, why should Roman Catholic weddings, like weddings in Anglican churches, be accepted as having a status in civil law when Muslim weddings don't?" [1]

Rowson's take certainly paints the Archbishop in a much more favourable light than the tabloids who would have us believe he was advocating a semi-Islamic state in Britain. However, I still believe that he is wrong to even hint at the prospect of any alteration of the law to accommodate religious jurisdiction as an alternative to the secular judiciary.

Once more, during the debate, there has been the usual outcry of "we are a Christian country". As I have stated before on this blog, that is not a label I accept for the UK (especially when we are comparing it to theocratic societies such as Iran.) Much of our legal system indeed reflects the Christian values of our leaders going back through history. But Britain's great strength is that it is a **free country**- where any citizen can follow the religion of choice, or indeed none at all. Notwithstanding the anachronism of the established CofE, all religions are treated with respect, but no one set of religious beliefs is given the force of law.

It is a central principle of our free and liberal society that all are equal under the law, and that is the Britain that I – and I believe many of my fellow citizens of all races and faiths- want to live in.

Thursday, 12 June 2008
Questions of Liberty ?

Year 9 Citizenship had a great opportunity yesterday, to get some really top-notch work from the learning objective *"Consider both sides of a topical debate."* Armed with a scene from *The Trial* (you've no idea how smug I was in the staffroom, telling colleagues I was doing **Kafka** with year 9), some material from the wake of **9/11**, and my trusty **BBC Briefing**, we went to work on the 42 days detention issue.

I hate sitting on the fence, but this is a tricky one.

In Labour Party conference a few years ago, Tony Blair rather worryingly dismissed "this Civil Liberties Nonsense.." which upset a lot of us (including, one would imagine, the former chair of the National Council for Civil Liberties- now our **Deputy Leader, Harriet Harman**.) Those of us on the democratic left actually **believe** in that nonsense, and have lost track of the number of tubes of *Bonjela* we ran through as a result of biting our tongues during the tenures of Charles Clarke and Jack Straw at the Home Office.

A core principle of British Law is the right to be **assumed to be innocent until proven guilty**. In some cases (murder, violent crime, etc) we have long accepted the detaining of suspects on remand, while the case is prepared, but only after they have been **formally charged**: ie. told by the police what they are being charged with !

In normal circumstances, any of us nicked by our friendly local copper can expect to be charged or released within **24 hours**. There have long been extensions for terrorist offences: during the troubles in Northern Ireland we managed with the option of (if I recall correctly) 7 days. Blair wanted 90, Parliament gave him 28. Seven terror suspects have been held up to that period since. But the evidence that 42 is needed remains sketchy. We know that MI5 don't want it, the police position is at best mixed, and it is unclear exactly who **plucked this figure from the sky**.

It is interesting to see how wholeheartedly the Tories have got into bed with Shami Chakrabarti and the Human Rights set. John O'Farrell's great book *Things Can Only Get Better* recalls the dismay of Labour activists when the Tories came tough in the first Gulf War. The Left had been denouncing Saddam for years as a tyrant, while the Thatcher government saw his as our unofficial ally, and sold him arms while he was at war with nasty-old Iran.

"Suddenly it seemed like the Conservatives had hijacked our baddie"[2]

And so with the Tories posture on this legislation. We all know that on the Tory benches are more than the fair share of **hang-em and flog-em right wingers**, and aside from them, a number of more thoughtful members who would consider **defence, national security and the fight against terror as their top priorities**. Yet, apart from Ann Widdecombe, all of the others fell into line behind "Call-me Dave" Cameron and his new lib-Cons. "Genghis" Clegg was happy to fall in line too- a rare opportunity for him to do something that looks faintly "liberal" rather than pushing for the abolition of the NHS. Norman Tebbit is likely to support the government in the House of Lords: **this is an issue he understands only too well** as his wife was horribly injured in the 1984 IRA Brighton Bomb.

The opinion polls suggest that the public are behind the tougher measure. Brown may well be banking on this being an area where Labour can seize the upper hand. It will be interesting to see how the public react, and especially, how the Tabloids run with it.

I still can't put my hand on my heart and tell you how I would have voted in last night's division. My gut instincts are that the principles of justice and law are too important to be discarded. Trevor Phillips- formerly an ultra-Blairite Labour loyalist, and now leader of the Equalities and Human Rights Commission, argued, on the basis of advice from Cherie Blair's Matrix Chambers, that:

"As the body charged with the promotion of human rights, we agree with ministers that the right to life is paramount, but that does not give us the liberty to take actions that unnecessarily violate other human rights. "Should the proposed measures be carried, the commission will immediately move to test its legality by launching a judicial review."[3]

On the other side, I remember what it felt like on September 11th 2001. I was doing my first teaching practice at a primary school in Eastbourne, and the world changed there and then. **The rules had changed, and so must our response.**

It was interesting (especially as I bang on constantly about "principles" to them) that my class of 13 and 14 year old students seemed more worried about the threat of terrorism than their rights being taken away (not even Kafka seemed to have an effect) I don't know if it was because their reasoning is more simple than that of the "adult" population, whether they reflected the views of their parents, or **whether their generation has been more conditioned to fight the "War on Terror" ?**

It was certainly the **spectre** of an outrage- maybe dwarfing our own so-called "7/7" - that Gordon Brown invoked this morning:

"I believe that the people who voted for this voted on principle because they are persuaded by the arguments. And I regret the fact that it was not possible to build a national consensus on this with the Conservative Party and I believe that they will regret their action in failing to support action that is necessary in our country to deal with both the causes and the problems associated with terrorism. And I would still appeal to them, and to other parties, to join the consensus that we need to take action to be prepared. And I do not want to have to come to the House of Commons and tell them that a terrorist incident has occurred, but we have not been properly prepared because we failed to take the legislative measures necessary."[4]

Monday 23 June 2008
Davis: That's NOT the way to do it...

As I said in my last post- the 42 days detention issue is a complicated one, and one where I struggle to come down on one side or other of the proverbial fence- mainly because when I'm about to, someone presents a compelling argument for the other side.

However, the David Davis farce provides a series of examples about "how not to do it"

Davis has resigned his seat in the House of Commons (actually only possible for applying for the nominal office of Steward of the Chiltern Hundreds, a position which disqualifies holders from sitting in Parliament.) The last time I am aware of this being used by an MP to re-fight their old seat on a point of principle was Bruce Douglas-Mann in 1982 when he defected from Labour to the SDP. It didn't, sadly, set a precedent for MPs defecting to other parties (whether Quentin Davies' Tory-Labour, Emma Nicholson's Tory-Lib Dem or Richard Balfe MEP's Labour –Tory road-to-Damascus style conversions)

Davies is resigning to re-fight his seat as a "referendum on civil liberties" - and there is much talk of defending British traditions: but it seems to avoid one glaring British tradition, that of **Parliamentary Democracy**.

Davies was elected by his constituents, on a platform, but, nonetheless as their representative first and foremost. He was elected to **apply his judgement to the issues** of government, as was every other MP, in a **Parliament of equals**. Decisions would be made by debate and then vote by those equal MPs. Even the role of Prime Minister actually rests on this principle: the post is held by whoever can command the majority of members of the House of Commons, regardless of what political party rules say (again, if you haven't read Chris Mullin's *A Very British Coup*, the fictitious election of Wainwright as Prime Minister over the supposed deputy leader of the Party illustrates exactly how the constitutional position works.)

The 42 days detention is law because the measure commanded the support of a majority of elected MPs in a democratic Parliament. (Genuine referenda have been used in a very limited way for what were considered changes to the Constitution: even these were subject to ratification by Parliament.)

A Tory MP standing in a safe Tory seat without being opposed by the nearest rivals ("Genghis" Clegg quite prepared to throw his lot in with the right-wing Tory) at a time when the Tories are massively ahead in the polls **is not an accurate referendum on the issue**. During the miners' strike, any coalfield Labour MP could have resigned to fight a by-election as a referendum on pit closures. They would have won hands down. Would Thatcher have listened? They could have resigned as a referendum on the Poll Tax. Would Thatcher have listened ? Of course not. She would have, quite rightly, seen it as an insult to the Mother of Parliaments and the Constitution (flawed, in my opinion, but that's another story) under which we are governed.

For the Tories to stand on a civil liberties platform would have seemed laughable a few years ago- as the party that turned miners away from the Dartford Tunnel, in case they were committing the heinous crime of going to Kent. The party that gave us the racist "sus" laws, or the homophobic Section 28. The party that introduced and renewed the Prevention of Terrorism Act, which, while not necessarily comparable to the 42 days, was certainly opposed by many of the same Labour rebels who opposed 42 days, on the same Civil Liberties grounds.

For the Lib Dems not to fight Davis seat is a glorious **tactical blunder**, for which their candidate in the next General election will curse loudly. They have secured Davis re-election next time by a massive majority.

For Labour not to fight the seat, I fear, may also prove a blunder. Damned if we do- this is a safe Tory seat where we are third. People who support 42 days (and I rather suspect that many of David Davis supporters are included in that) will not bring themselves to vote for "the socialists". We would come resoundingly second, and that would be used as a **propaganda victory** in the debate about 42 days (which, if we think our democracy is worth upholding, is a debate that should have ended in Parliament after the vote.) Damned if we don't- as we will be seen as cowardlily refusing to stand up for the policy passed in our name.

The **independent candidate** idea is an interesting one- but not the name originally touted (by himself.) **Kelvin McKenzie**, erstwhile editor of *The Sun* declared his candidacy on This Week, and suggested that **Rupert Murdoch** would financially back him (not actually allowed, as the "Dirty Digger" has a US passport) McKenzie declared himself to be fully behind 42 days- indeed that he would **prefer 420 days**. Unfortunately, this right-wing, union-bashing, sexist, xenophobic, homophobic lowest-common-denominator lout is best remembered by Labour supporters for Kinnock's head in a light bulb in April 1992, exhorting "Will the last person to leave Britain please turn the lights out", and crowing **"It was the Sun wot won it!"** after Major's surprise re-election. **It is as unlikely that Labour supporters who back 42 days could bring themselves to vote for this creature as it is that pro-42 day Tories would vote Labour.**

Northampton market trader Eamonn Fitzpatrick is the nearest thing to a 42 day candidate, but is even less well known than the few others in the race- including **The Mad Cow Girl**, and **Miss Great Britain**. **David Icke** has also, apparently, expressed an interest.

If there is a genuinely independent pro-42 day candidate, then the result could indeed be interesting. But in the absence of one (and, frankly, no names spring to mind) it will be an **expensive farce- and the taxpayers of Haltenprice, and Parliamentary Democracy, will both be poorer as a result.**

Monday, 20 October 2008
Doctor Death in Eastbourne

In a week where the assisted suicide of former rugby player Daniel James was headline news, Eastbourne narrowly escaped playing host to **"Dr Death" Philip Nitschke** of the group *Exit International*, who holds seminars on how people can take their own life.

It is not often that I agree with Colin Belsey (indeed, I think this is only the second time on this blog) but the decision of the Langham Hotel to cancel his booking is **absolutely right**. The police confirmed that there were doubts about the legality of the seminars:

"There is legislation against this sort of thing and offences may have been committed if people were being told how to end their lives," Chief Inspector Coates of Eastbourne Police told the Eastbourne Herald [5]

As a (liberal) Christian, my personal feelings are against assisted suicide, but I accept that this is a huge issue, and one that requires a wide debate in a calm and rational way. Such a debate needs to be had urgently: but those such as Dr Nitschke should not seek to second-guess the outcome of such a debate.

The right to life is enshrined in the **International Declaration of Human Rights**. At what point does the right to decide when to end life come into force ? The case of Diane Pretty , a MND sufferer who went to the European Court to determine whether she had the right to end her life with dignity while she still had capacity was an agonising one, but came down against endorsing a right to suicide. Diane had written:

"I want to have a quick death without suffering, at home surrounded by my family so that I can say good-bye to them."[6]

In a counter argument in the same article, Rachel Hurst, director of **Disability Awareness in Action**, said it would be:

"very wrong for justice to say in certain circumstances people can die...It would be a slippery slope and many people who did not want to die could be affected,"[7]

We already have a number of legal rights in this area. Many cancer patients exercise the right to **refuse treatments** that would prolong their life- often with very disturbing side-effects. Patients with terminal illness have the right to request that they are **not artificially resuscitated**. My own grandmother was able to slip away peacefully in her own bed, having expressed the wish **not to be taken into hospital** when the end came.

The right to die with dignity is undisputed. Whether this extends to granting the legal right for a life to be artificially terminated is far less clear. I look forward to the debate happening, and fully expect to have my own opinions challenged, and maybe even altered. **But the place to do that is through our democratic parliament, and not in seminars at the seaside.**

ARTY TIME

I never brought myself to write "Actor" on forms under "occupation," but I did study drama for three years, and do a bit of paid work in the theatre. Rather predictably, my later encounters with the industry were as Secretary of the local Equity union branch.

Since moving from drama dreams to drama teaching, I have nonetheless kept up my interest in the world of the Arts- as these columns reflect.

Sunday, 17 June 2007
Anyone for a day out ? It'll cost you...

The Tories are already planning where their massive tax-cutting agenda will hit first, and museums and galleries are in line. The Daily Torygraph reported today that the Conservatives would:

"end the Government's policy of automatic free entry and allow institutions to levy a charge for admission" [1]

Now, while many people would consider this a minor issue in the great scheme of things, Teacher Dave leaps in to defend the free admission. There are several reasons for this.

First, I agreed with Tony Blair's mantra of "education, education, education" and this shouldn't stop at school. Life-long Learning has been around as a buzz-phrase for a long time, and long may it continue. We don't stop widening and improving our knowledge and ideas at 16 or 18 or 21.

Secondly, the collections in the museums and galleries mentioned belong to "us" the nation. Furthermore, they all benefit from significant public funding, whether from the taxpayer or indirectly through the lottery. How far this can be justified when they also have (from what I remember under the Tories) significant admission charges.

Thirdly, the policy of free entry has been a huge success. The Torygraph published figures showing that "in London, visits to formerly charging museums have risen by 86 per cent. Elsewhere, there has been an increase of 75 per cent".[2]

Far from abolishing this policy, our leaders need to look at how accessible other publicly funded arts and cultural institutions are. An old bugbear of mine is the Royal Opera House. This is, quite rightly, a national treasure, producing productions of the highest quality. To do this, it has to milk public funds profusely. Yet ticket prices remain out of reach for many ordinary families (and school parties !) who would appreciate access to what is wrongly seen as an elitist art form.

The museums remain a source of enrichment for millions, and have much to teach some of our other education institutions. My mum, a pensioner, regularly attended evening classes in art at Sussex Downs College (for which she paid, with no complaint.) Recently, she was annoyed to discover that, as well as the practical teaching, she was expected to write "essays" so that the course could be "properly accredited".

Is our vision of lifelong learning really so narrow, that we don't believe that our pensioners (many who are already highly qualified) can seek to learn and develop new skills without having to sit exams or do coursework to get the bit of paper to add to their (also retired !) CV ?

When I trained as a teacher, "What is Education For?" was a popular topic for discussion. We clearly still need to answer it!

Saturday 24 May 2008
Radical Lewes

Did you know that, deep in conservative (and mainly Conservative) East Sussex, lies a spirit of dissent, radicalism, hope and solidarity? No, neither did I until recently. It comes in the shape of the **Radical Lewes** Festival.

Lewes certainly has a radical past- as home of Thomas Paine, the author of Rights of Man; as the location of a famous Protestant Martyrdom under Bloody Mary, and home to many socialists and left thinkers over the years. So it's reassuring to see that the fire still, occasionally, burns bright and red. All events in the festival are FREE, and include:

WOODY GUTHRIE 'HARD TIMES AND HARD TRAVELLIN': a live musical programme based on the life of the radical American songster, with historical commentary by Dr. Will Kaufmann.

THE LEGACY OF ROBERT TRESSELL: discussion with Billy Hayes, Gen.Secretary of the Postal Workers' Union, and John McDonnell MP- the man who tried unsuccessfully to challenge Gordon Brown for the Labour leadership, and others. Robert Tressell was the Hastings based author of the novel The Ragged Trousered Philanthropists- essential socialist reading.

ROBERT TRESSELL'S HASTINGS: A guided walk by the chair of Lewes Labour Party, Trevor Hopper, around the Hastings sites featured in The Ragged Trousered Philanthropists. Not part of the Radical Lewes Festival, but well worth taking part.   And the highlight of the festival...

SUSSEX AND THE SPANISH CIVIL WAR: an evening of contemporary prose, poetry and song, devised by Mike Anderson and featuring Bill Thorneycroft (eyewitness) , Marlene Sidaway (National Theatre), Jim Jump (editor, 'Poems from Spain'), and the legendary Jack Jones. Jack, now 95, was the leader of the TGWU in the 1970's having been a volunteer in the International Brigades who went to fight against fascism in the Spanish Civil War. There are only a handful of these brave old men still alive: there will not be many more opportunities to hear their testimony.

Note: Should adverts for past events appear in a book like this ? When the events were this good- then yes!

Monday 23 June 2008
Then and Now

Following my appearance with Jack Jones at the Spanish Civil War event, it occurred to me that I hadn't seen Jack for ten years- the last time was at a Labour fundraiser in Eastbourne in 1999. It was a race night at the TGWU centre, and Jack was there as President of the National Pensioners' Convention. Who's changed the most, I wonder ?

Monday, 23 June 2008
Solidaridad

It is 70 years since the start of the **Spanish Civil War**, when a democratically elected Left-wing government in Spain was challenged and eventually overthrown in a **fascist coup-d'état**, led by General Franco.

Franco received **material and military support from Nazi Germany and Fascist Italy** (the Nazi Condor Legion honed the bombing skills they would use a few years later in the Blitz, by practicing on undefended civilians at **Guernica**) There was even support from within the British establishment (Franco was flown from the Canary Islands to Morocco at the start of the uprising by a British MI6 operative who, believe it or not, set off from Croydon Airport !)

As the official Republican Government faltered, their cause was bolstered by the volunteer **International Brigades**: socialists, trade unionists and anti-fascist activists from all over the world, who joined up to fight for the Republicans against Franco's fascists. Many volunteered from Britain- a significant number from Sussex: including **Harry Turner**, a Labour Party activist from Polegate, who died in the late 1980's.

Over 4,000 children, mainly from the Basque region fled to Britain, and many were settled in Sussex. Michael Portillo's **grossly distorted** documentary tells how these niños were looked after by the churches and the boy scouts. In fact, the refugee effort was run by Communists, Labour left wingers, co-operators and trades unionists, whose efforts shamed the churches and other liberal groups on board- but Portillo, himself the son of a "dirty red" conveniently forgets this…

I was privileged to take part in an event hosted by **Lewes Trades Council**, that celebrated the sacrifices made by Sussex folk to aid the International Brigades.

In a multi-arts event written by Mike Anderson, I joined with Dave Mottley (of NASUWT, but we don't hold that against him) and his band, and a variety of other readers and performers, including the son of veteran Jim Jump, and the brother of veteran Chris Thorneycroft, who read their relatives original words. There was music, poetry and audience song, and an opening address by former TGWU union leader **Jack Jones**- now 95- and one of the few remaining veterans.

An audience of well over 100 packed into Southover Church Hall, and thoroughly enjoyed this piece of living history. It was interesting to reflect upon what effect a defeat of Franco's fascists might have had in the war on fascist Germany and Italy- whatever your conclusions, we should salute the sacrifices made by those principled men (and women) who went to Spain, either as soldiers or other activists, including those who never returned.

Wednesday, 6 August 2008
Arty Time

It's been quite an artsy couple of weeks- having enjoyed the Rattonians' visually stunning ***Copacabana***, and the array of work (so far) as part of my good friend and colleague Steve Scott's **Shakespeare Experience**- to date: a fantastic evening at **Louise Jameson's** one-woman show ***Through Women's Eyes*** (collection of Shakespeare monologues for women, interspersed with stories from Louise's distinguished past) then the result of a week's intense work with Louise by a group of young performers in ***Wotcha Will***- another superb "best of the Bard" piece; and then topped off with ***An Audience With Colin Baker***- a man with a virtual treasury of stories from a long career (and not just the years when he was playing "him")

I have worked with Steve for many years- our company ***Grassy Knoll*** put on a number of quality fringe productions, and on some occasions were lucky to secure some grant funding. This, however is getting tighter, and, the conventional wisdom goes, the only projects that will be funded between now and 2013 will be those that **incorporate five rings** into the project somehow....

The quality of a civilisation can be measured by its arts: **its theatre, literature, music, etc**. We had our arguments about this in the 1980's: **Norman Tebbit** was a fearsome critic of the Arts Council and the **very principle** of state funding for arts projects (the Thatcherites believed that the "Market" would solve everything) Margaret Thatcher herself was more accommodating, but made no secret of her dislike for the **National Theatre**- our only really well funded producer of challenging drama. She made just one visit to a production during her time in office: ***Amadeus***, where she berated the director, Sir Peter Hall, for his and Peter Shaffer's (historically accurate) interpretation of the great composer...

"She was not pleased. In her best headmistress style, she gave me a severe wigging for putting on a play that depicted Mozart as a scatological imp with a love of four-letter words. It was inconceivable, she said, that a man who wrote such exquisite and elegant music could be so foul mouthed. I said that Mozart's letters proved he was just that: he had an extraordinarily infantile sense of humour. In a sense, he protected himself from maturity by indulging his childishness. **'I don't think you heard what I said,' replied the Prime Minister. 'He couldn't have been like that'.**

" I offered (and sent) a copy of Mozart's letters to Number Ten the next day; I was even thanked by the appropriate Private Secretary. But it was useless: the Prime Minster said I was wrong, so wrong I was."[3]

The former Tory MP **Terry Dicks** bemoaned the very existence of arts funding – paying for "someone prancing around in a box": his attack on this in the House of Commons was countered by the late champion of the arts **Tony Banks**, who opined that *"it was proof that a pig's bladder on a stick can get elected to Parliament"* (When the Speaker questioned whether that was appropriate Parliamentary language, Banks pointed out *"It's artistic, Mr Speaker"*)[4]

Earlier this year, my old union *Equity* passed a motion of "no confidence" in the Arts Council of England, at a packed meeting in London, including stars such as Kevin Spacey. They were, rightly, protesting that the funding carpet was being pulled from a number of established theatres and other groups- who had enjoyed modest success, but were not viable without some public subsidy. **Yet, the real challenge comes further down.**

The small grants to regional and local groups may not be in the same league as the £20+ million for the Royal Opera House, but it is these that give the many and varied opportunities to our young people to experience, enjoy, and explore their cultural identities. The move from the Arts Council seems to suggest that funding will only get you up and running, and then it has to be "commercial".

The *Shakespeare Experience* projects (and two more still to come- *Romeo and Juliet* and *Lear's Daughters*) could only be commercially viable with massive private sponsorship or a fee to the participants that would be prohibitive to many ordinary families. Even now, there are precious few opportunities for the participants to develop their skills during the rest of the year: the established groups are loathe to stray from the "big musicals" path, as even one poorly supported show could signal the end. Credit to them, it gets people involved and gets people into our theatres: but where do they go **next**- where's the next step up ? The challenges ?

Government in the 21st century needs to look at how real **grassroots arts strategies** can deliver breadth, diversity, and creative innovation in the coming years: the pursuit of excellence, not just the commercial safety of the lowest common denominator.

Friday 15 August 2008
Lessons from the cinema ?

The arty theme continues, as I was also lucky enough last week to get along to see the superb film *Cass* (making me a rarity in Eastbourne, as it involved a late night drive to **Crawley** for the privilege.) My original reason for making the journey had been because the film features my friend and former student Jayson Wheatley, (who plays one of the main characters "when they were younger",) however, it left me wondering why this compelling British movie did not enjoy the wide release it deserved

Cass tells the **true story** of Cass Pennant, a black lad adopted by white parents in the 1950's, and growing up in the then predominantly white working-class East end. Cass is attracted by the sense of belonging through following a football club, and becomes involved in one of the "firms" of organised football hooligans that characterised that period in the late 1970's and early 80's.

Cass rises to become one of the leading organisers of a West Ham firm, ultimately ending up serving a severe jail sentence. On his release, he finds a new and successful career supervising the doors of nightclubs in London's roughest areas *(including Lewisham... I used to live there....)* However, the ghosts of the past are still present, and surface in a number of dramatic twists- which I won't tell you as you need to go and see the film yourself *(or get it when it comes out on DVD.)*

Cass is an **important piece of recent social history**. Young football fans in the family-friendly atmosphere of today may not realise just how far the game has come. The culture of violence permeated the game in the 1980's- with many other "firms" like those in the film sprung up- attached to all the big clubs (and a few smaller ones as well) **Far-right groups** like the National Front infiltrated many of these- a number of the current BNP top brass have **convictions for football hooliganism**. The most significant incident was the 1985 Heysel Stadium disaster, in which 39 fans died, and, as a result, English clubs were banned from all European tournaments (a ban not lifted for five years)

A wide ranging enquiry into football by Judge Popplewell the same year concluded ominously: *"football may not be able to continue in its present form much longer"* [5]

The determination of the government to tackle the problem, coupled with the wide reaching **Taylor Report** that followed the Hillsborough Stadium disaster (which was **not** in any way hooligan related) brought in a range of provisions to clean up the game. Additionally, following Hillsborough, the terraces were replaced by all-seater stadia, and the perimeter fences were removed. **Racist chanting** was specifically criminalised, and fans groups (such as *Show Racism the Red Card*, and Manchester United supporters' anti-fascist organisation *Red Attitude*) challenged some of the issues of racist and fascist involvement in organised violence.

Can we learn from the manner in which a **whole culture** was changed ?

The fans themselves, supported, but not directed by political leaders on all sides, were able to completely alter the culture around the game. By making the hooligan culture **socially unacceptable**, and fostering a determination to remove the perpetrators of gang violence from the game (including the imposition of long, or even life, bans from their chosen club) football was taken back for the law-abiding fans and for the family.

Of course, things aren't perfect, but they're a far cry from where we were in the '80s. Could we learn lessons from the demise of the football hooligan culture in tackling the current plague of **knife crime** in our cities ? Certainly any ratcheting up of punishments will only have an effect if it is alongside a concerted effort to **stigmatise knife-carrying amongst the impressionable young people who currently accept it as a way of life**.

(Interestingly, Jayson also popped up in an advertising campaign trying to do exactly that: if you saw the "not a good look" ads on MTV and elsewhere, he was the guy in the orange suit.)

If you get a chance to see **Cass** (and indeed similar films like ***Green Street***) then do so- pieces of our recent social history- and who knows, maybe we can learn something from it…

TRANSPORT

Getting about. One of those second- tier political issues in any campaign, but actually one of the most important day-to-day services that so many of us rely on. Whether it's the issue of the free bus passes (introduced by Labour, by the way) or the privatized rail system, or the state of roads, it is always a subject that generated public interest.

During the life of the column, Eastbourne Borough Council sold off the world's oldest publicly-owned bus company- Eastbourne Buses, bringing transport issues into some of the final editions.

Sunday, 19 August 2007
U-turn if you want: the Tory's not for turning

Nigel Waterson is being his usual evasive self about the pay-to-park scheme being imposed on Eastbourne by the Tory County Council. He has avoided a direct challenge by local businessman calling for him to listen to the views of local Chamber of Commerce, Federation of Small Business, the ruling group on Eastbourne Borough Council, and many local residents who are against this.

The Parking scheme was a huge issue in the local elections- the Liberal Democrats campaigned strongly against (although proposed one that was not dissimilar last time they were in power locally !) The Eastbourne Tories, under their now defeated leader Ian Lucas assured us that they were against... well parts of it, at least - and certainly spun things to make them sound opposed:

"We are still in there fighting Eastbourne's corner — we are closer to the needs of Eastbourne than the county council," and:

"There will be a cost, but it should be a fair cost not over the top. If that can be achieved, it's a good thing. If we can't achieve that the borough council will not contribute to the scheme."[1]

Well, once their disastrous (from 15 councillors to 7) election campaign was out of the way, a chance for the Eastbourne Tories on the county council to really "fight Eastbourne's corner". In a motion tabled by the Lib Dems, (who had, in fairness, made scrapping the scheme a central plank of their policies- and won the election handsomely) the County Council was asked to scrap the parking scheme. How did the "listening" Tory councillors vote ?

DAVID ELKIN: New leader of the Conservative group (rump- there's 7 of them) on Eastbourne Borough, and Lucas' deputy in May- voted AGAINST scrapping the scheme.
BARRY TAYLOR: Meads county councillor- a role he repeats as one of their borough councillors- voted AGAINST scrapping the scheme.
MICHAEL TUNWELL: Ratton county councillor and recent Mayor of Eastbourne- our former "first citizen" of the borough- voted AGAINST scrapping the scheme.
BOB LACEY: One of the high profile scalps of May 3rd- lost his usually safe Upperton seat on the borough, but remains their County Councillor..... well Bob abstained, but as Chairman of the County Council (similar to our

Mayor) would not be expected to come into play unless there was a tie. I wonder how he would have used his casting vote?

Eastbourne Labour Party has written to the Secretary of State for Transport, urging her to veto the project, although some construction work is already underway. We're not against some parking control, but the massive scale of the on-street parking goes way beyond Eastbourne's needs. I'll leave it to local businessman David Cooper to sum up, as he did so eloquently in this week's Eastbourne Herald:

"I believe that a parking scheme is needed. That is beyond all reasonable doubt. But what is needed is one that is effective and achieves that with the lowest capital cost outlay and one that won't need ongoing money thrown at it and will need to increase in cost as the effectiveness takes hold. The scheme that is currently proposed needs huge capital sums expended, and will need ongoing maintenance, repair, amendment when prices increase, will need a power supply to operate etc all at a cost. All the town needs is a few traffic wardens to increase the risk of offenders being caught." [2]

The campaign goes on...

Saturday, 19 July 2008
Take back the track

In the dying days of the last Tory government, the headless chickens and (according to their own leader) "bastards" in the Major Cabinet decided that the way to win back public support was to try and be **really, really like Thatcher**, and privatise something. Even if this was something that was an **essential public** service, that would always need taxpayer subsidy, and was acknowledged by almost everybody – **even your own side**- as a bad idea for selling off.

Plan A was the Post Office. I had just joined the Labour Party, and stood with local stalwarts such as the late Terry Page outside Willingdon Triangle Post Office collecting signatures and giving out stickers saying *"You'll Miss the Post"*. It was a brilliant campaign by Labour, alongside the Communication Workers Union (back in the days when Alan Johnson was a trade unionist…) and the plans were withdrawn.

Plan B was to sell off the railways.

The splitting up and selling off of individual rail lines produced no end of material for the comedians of Britain. **Virgin Trains** became the butt of most transport gags, whilst, in my neck of the woods, **Connex** became a general word for anything that you didn't like (it is a pity that they lost their franchise: I have been trying to persuade the kids I teach not to use the word "gay" as a catch-all term for something rubbish, and the rail regulator robbed me of an obvious alternative suggestion.) **Less funny was the hike in fares, the drop in standards and the cutting of services that followed.**

I was at Labour Party conference in 1995, to hear Tony Blair promise that there would be **"a publicly accountable and publicly owned rail network under a Labour government"** Sadly, this was one of many throwbacks to socialism that Blair was cured of by the likes of Doctor Mandelson and co. on coming to power (at the same conference the education spokesman **David Blunkett** declared: "Read my lips- no selection by interview or exam under a Labour government" …)

Rail privatisation came to a partial end in 2002 when **Railtrack**- the privately floated company set up to manage the track, went bust. The ultra-Blairite Stephen Byers was transport secretary at the time, and, while he made it clear that the new Network Rail was as far from a renationalisation as was possible, it did, at least take the management of track back into something like the public sector, albeit as a private company accountable to government. The veteran Labour minister Jack Straw proudly celebrated this fact in ringingly Old Labour terms last year, telling the House:

"... rail privatisation ... was one of the most catastrophic reorganisations, which we have had to resolve, and having done that — [Interruption.] The hon. Member for Wellingborough (Mr. Bone) may mock, but we brought **Network Rail into public ownership ...**" [3]

The campaign by the **Co-Operative Party** *(which has an electoral agreement with Labour)* goes one step further, in calling for Network Rail to become a **mutual company**. This would allow passengers and the interested public to become equal shareholders, to elect the board and to hold the management accountable. Given the huge bonuses that managers still received the year that Railtrack went bust- this has got to be a good thing. It is **not renationalisation**, and doesn't relate to the train operators, but would be an acknowledgement of the need for an accountable and service-focused rail system !

Monday 12 January 2009
On the buses

Even in my "Everything's gone too mad to blog" time, I managed to slip a letter or two into the Eastbourne Herald regarding the Lib Dems' sale of our century-old public bus company to transport giant Stagecoach...

LETTER FROM DAVE TO THE EASTBOURNE HERALD, 14th November 2008:

The people of Eastbourne were the first in the country to own their own bus company, and for over a century have been proud of this facility. It is ironic that, symptomatic perhaps of their lurch to the right under Nick Clegg, it is a Liberal Democrat council that is privatising this piece of Eastbourne residents' property.

Successive councils have missed the chance to strengthen and develop Eastbourne Buses as both a profitable and a socially responsible concern. Opportunities to give a real say in the running of our bus company to passengers and other stakeholders will now be lost forever.

I find myself in the unusual position of agreeing with Nigel Waterson's call for the Lib Dem (bargain basement ?) sell-off to be halted, and for a real investigation into how the town can maintain and improve a viable bus company, preferably still owned by the people of Eastbourne.

Yours
Dave Brinson

LETTER FROM DAVE IN THE EASTBOURNE HERALD, 28th November 2008

I was disappointed that your editorial last week reduced the debate about the future of Eastbourne Buses to "the colour of the livery". The fact is that this debate is absolutely about services (and fares) in our community.

An Eastbourne-based company has this town as its sole focus: selling out to one of the big companies reduces us to one small part of a large, profit-driven transport operation. A council-owned Eastbourne Buses is obliged by law to operate on a commercial basis, and preferably to return a modest profit. However, under local ownership, that profit can be invested back into the company rather than into private shareholders' pockets.

The council certainly needed to take a serious look at the management of Eastbourne Buses: as any private operator will also need to do. But a local public ownership is far less likely to make the savage service cuts, fare increases or attacks on drivers'
pensions that seem inevitable if there is a bargain basement sell-off to a private operator .

A really radical council would have looked at the whole business structure of the company, and considered how a genuinely Eastbourne-owned company could best serve the community. Perhaps looking at successful co-operative community business models, involving passengers and residents in decision making could have saved the company, rather than years of simply providing the chance for a handful of local councillors to add "company director" to their CV !

It seems that the Lib Dems have done the deal to flog this piece of Eastbourne residents' property: a sad end to over 100 years of our history.

Yours
Dave Brinson

Clearly we helped to get the debate going: I was heartened to read a supportive letter the following week from a regular correspondent to the Herald, Edward Thomas. Mr Thomas and I do not always agree on issues, but on this he is spot on.

ONE WORLD: OUR WORLD

As a socialist, I am proud to enjoy many identities- British, English, Eastbournian, ex-pat Londoner, European... But most importantly, I am proud to be a global citizen: a citizen of the World.

Any civilized person needs to take an interest not just in what is going on in their own back yard, or even their own country, but on this fragile planet we all share. I am proud to have always been involved in international organizations tackling poverty, lack of education, human rights abuses and climate change across the globe.

1998 also saw the great hope of the Obama victory in the USA. As the columns reveal, I was terrified that it wouldn't happen: isn't it great to be wrong sometimes!

Saturday, 14 July 2007
Breaking Sweat

Congratulations are due to the young campaigners who organised the Breaking Sweat event at the Eastbourne Underground Theatre last night.

I was unable to stay for the concert, but bought my ticket and went down to show support- not really needed from me, as there was a packed house, to see a variety of performers, including the fabulous Gunpowder Plot, and dance numbers from Ratton students.

Jamie Finden and his team have worked really hard to raise awareness of the scandalous issue of sweatshop labour, and it's an area where the Government needs to listen to their work, supported by many individual politicians, trade unions and charities.

The decision of Top Shop to introduce an ethical clothing range is welcome on the surface but will prove to be nothing more than a cynical marketing ploy unless more action is taken to persuade and pressurise the bigger manufacturers to respect workers' rights.

The power of the consumer is going to be an increasing political force in coming years, and all the Parties avoid it at their peril. In the spirit of cross-party action, it was good to see the ubiquitous Lib Dem campaigner Stephen Lloyd at the event, and a number of Green Party supporters. Less pleasing was the big stall from a (very) thinly-disguised front organisation of the Militant Tendency (sorry…."Socialist Party of Britain"…) who seem to have rediscovered the old zeal for getting their talons into any broad political campaign- a bit like ants in these warm months…

Nonetheless, to see so many young people being so politicized about such an important world issue is one in the eye for the whining media commentators who write off the young generation as not being bothered. All power to Jamie and his fellow campaigners, and let's see more of it!

Monday, 6 August 2007
Ending the genocide

In the week when Gordon Brown met up with George "Dubya" Bush and showed the President that he was more interested in discussing world affairs than the unscheduled ride in the President's golf buggy, Britain becomes one of the leading players in a global effort to end the genocide in Darfur.

Since rebels took up arms in the region, in the west of Nigeria, the rebels and (unofficially pro-government) Janjaweed fighters, have burned and pillaged villages in a campaign that has created more than 200,000 refugees.

A ceasefire negotiated in 2004, and policed by the African Union has been woefully inadequate, and the UN has described the situation as one of the worst humanitarian crisis in the world.

Following a Security Council resolution on 31st July, Over 25,000 troops and international police have now been sent to the region to protect civilians and aid workers. Burkina Faso, Nigeria, Egypt, Cameroon and Ethiopia have all pledged troops, which should ensure that (in contrast to the peacekeeping efforts in Iraq) the operation is seen as being an African delivered solution, rather than simply the "West" muscling in.

Gordon Brown makes a good start as an international statesman, and, hopefully, if UNAMID (United Nations- African Union Mission In Darfur) is a success, it will herald a return to internationalism in peacekeeping and security- what the late Robin Cook memorably described as an ethical foreign policy.

Friday, 28 December 2007
They must not prevail

The assassination of any political figure is a despicable assault on democracy, but few have been potentially more damaging than the assassination of Benazir Bhutto in Pakistan yesterday.

The assassination of Bhutto is not simply the murder of a politician. The Bhuttos have been referred to as Pakistan's Kennedys- her father was a populist prime minister in the 1970's before being deposed and executed in another coup. Bhutto served as Prime Minister twice- the first woman to be elected to lead any Islamic nation in the world.

As one of the most influential Islamic states, and the only one to be a declared nuclear power, a stable Pakistan is crucial in maintaining peace in this volatile region. The ideal would be a fully democratic Pakistan (something we've seen on and off since its independence) governed by a moderate and secular government.

In 1999, General Musharraf's coup overthrew the democratic government of Nawaz Sharif, and dismissed the elected legislative assembly. Initially, the world treated Musharraf's coup as it would any other military takeover of a democracy- the Commonwealth promptly expelled it from membership. However, attitudes have softened towards Pakistan since 2001, when Musharraf became an outspoken critic of Islamic extremism, and an ally in the so-called War on Terror. In 2005, he spoke to an audience of Jewish leaders in New York- unthinkable even a few years before.

It was clear that Musharraf's place as a trusted ally of the West was conditional, in the long term, upon moves to restore Pakistan as a democracy, and moves such as his transformation into an (apparently) non-military President sped up this process. However, the imposition of a state of emergency threatened to undermine the progress made. So, the return of Bhutto to contest the forthcoming elections gave the clearest indication of an intention to complete the transition to full and legitimate democracy.

Pakistan is currently in three days of official mourning, during which it is likely to become apparent what the next stage of the electoral process will be. Will the elections continue, or will we see a return to the state of emergency and democracy put on the back burner once again?

It is vital that the latter is not allowed to happen. If we want to see a democratic Pakistan, and the spread of democracy around the globe, then the terrorists cannot be seen to have won.

Prime Minister Gordon Brown condemned the attacks as a "cowardly attack" and stated:

"The international community is united in its outrage and determination that those who stoop to such tactics shall not prevail,"[1]

They must not prevail.

Wednesday, 6 February 2008
America decides

The choice of the next President of the United States is entirely the prerogative of the citizens of that country. However, as the world's largest economy and strongest military (and diplomatic?) power, it is only to be expected that politicos like myself take an interest.

The centre of the US political spectrum tends to sit considerably to the Right of Europe- hence the oddity of many British Tories who support the Democratic Party (I recall Alan Duncan speaking of his hopes for John Kerry on the eve of the last presidential election), while us Labour supporters often find our nearest political kinsman in the US displaying a moderation (if not an overt conservatism) that makes Tony Blair look dangerously left wing....

This time round, however, there is a real hope that the Democrats could display a bit of progressive (dare I even say "Left") thinking. Both Clinton and Obama are committed to introducing some form of universal healthcare, which, while not necessarily creating NHS:USA, will end the scandal of millions of citizens in the richest nation on earth going without decent medical protection. Both Clinton and Obama are committed to supporting international responses to climate change and internationalism generally. Both support partnership rights for gay and lesbian people (although don't you dare call it "marriage", they still say....) and both support a woman's right to choose to terminate her pregnancy. Both have been supported by a range of American Labor (trade) unions, suggesting good times ahead for workplace rights (although the most pro-union candidate appeared to be John Edwards who crashed out of the race after an encouraging start in Iowa, where he beat Hillary.)

As our good friends at Facebook have an application that allows members to display their favourite Presidential Candidate, I took advantage and displayed my endorsement of Ohio Congressman Dennis Kucinich. This wasn't because I agreed with everything he said, or even thought he was electable in a country as conservative as the States, but because he was throwing things into the debate that the "moderates" were scared of raising- for instance
- Abolishing the Death Penalty
- Stronger Gun Control
- Free pre-school and college level education
- Full Social Security benefits at 65
- Legalising same sex marriage

- Creating a balance between workers and corporations, and- most importantly of all....
- Fostering a world of international co-operation

Kucininch crashed out of the race after poor performances in the early primaries, and a battle with NBC after they decided to drop him from the televised debate in South Carolina. In fairness, Kucinich and the other low-budget contenders suffered a virtual media blackout in a country where political TV advertising is an established part of the process, and the cult of "personality" is rife.

John Edwards had the dubious privilege of being my Facebook favourite for all of 48 hours, before he withdrew. So I'm reluctant to express a preference for Hillary or Barak, in the knowledge that, on current form, whoever I back is likely to lose!

But, with the Republican party pushed to the fringes of the Right, and riven by factional religious divides (Evangelical Christians are backing Huckabee, Mormons are backing Romney, and both are attacking each other; while divorce, gay rights and abortion made Rudy Giuliani a hate figure for many on the religious Right, ironically destroying the chances of the most moderate and able candidate in the Republican race) it looks likely that America will elect either its first woman or first black president. (If not, and McCain pulls it off, it will a blow against ageism- as he will be America's oldest president)

However it goes, November 2008 will be one to watch- the result is guaranteed to be a "first"

Friday, 21 March 2008
A land fit for heroes

It's not a phrase that you will see often on this blog, but **Nick Clegg is right**.

He is, of course wrong about many things- breaking up the NHS, opposing rights for agency workers, trying to prevent elected MPs from having a say on the EU constitutional treaty etc.

But he's right about the Gurkhas.

These elite Nepali soldiers have been an integral part of the British Army for nearly 200 years, and there has been fierce competition amongst young men (and women, since 2006) to sign up to serve. Gurkha troops have formed part of the British contingent in all of the major campaigns in that time- including recently in Afghanistan, where they served alongside Prince Harry.

I have a strong personal interest in the Gurkhas, as my mother spent three years as a Civilian Attached teacher with the Royal Gurkha Rifles in Malaya in the early 1960's, shortly after the emergency- and she can vouch first-hand for the bravery and commitment of these soldiers.

The Gurkhas serve between 15 and 30 years, currently based in Folkestone, Kent. For some years now, there have been campaigns to recognise the gross injustices of the pension (six times lower) for Gurkha servicemen, and especially the widows' pensions for the wives and families of those who have made the ultimate sacrifice for Britain. I am proud that the Labour Government has at least partially dealt with this injustice- Gurkha servicemen who retired after 1997 will receive the same pension as their British counterparts.

The current campaign, however, hinges on the issue of British Citizenship. Gurkhas who retire want the right to claim British Citizenship and the right to live in the country they have served- often for decades. Those who retired after 1997 have the automatic right to remain in the country, but older veterans have to apply. The logic of that date is, as Gordon Brown told the House of Commons, the year that the official base for the Gurkhas became mainland Britain, from the former British Colony of Hong Kong. However, I feel that this misses the point, not least because most Gurkha veterans will have served the British people across the globe- and if anything is worthy of attracting "earned" British citizenship, that would be it (it's certainly one better than proving that you know who Mr Speaker is, and what to do if you spill somebody's pint, as asked in the new Citizenship Test...)

We did the right thing over pensions and citizenship for post-1997 Gurkha veterans, now we just need Gordon to complete the task, by giving that practical acknowledgement of the debt we owe to what is a small number of courageous and selfless heroes. He should take heed from British commander Sir Ralph Turner MC, speaking in 1931:

"Bravest of the brave, most generous of the generous, never had a country more faithful friends than you"[2]

Gurkha Soldiers pictured serving Britain back in 1896.

Monday 15 September 2008
Eyes on America

William Hague has attacked Gordon Brown for hinting that he might support Barak Obama's quest for the White House. Hague said:

"A responsible British prime minister needs to be ready to work with either presidential candidate after the U.S. election, and should neither take sides nor be seen to be taking sides,"[5]

Surely this can't be William Hague of the same Tory party who had one **John McCain** as a **keynote speaker** at their conference just two years ago ? The same Tory party who had **Republican governor Arnold Schwarzeneger** speaking about his brand of conservatism? The Tory party that routinely sends its bright young things over to work for the **US Republican Party** as interns and researchers?

Labour and the US Democrats have always had a strong and very public relationship. **Bill Clinton** wowed the Labour conference a few years back: he had reasons to be grateful, as British Labour strategists **advised Clinton** in 1992 based on our bitter experiences of losing the General election earlier that year. Clinton went on to storm to the Presidency.

The US Republican party that gave us 8 years of Bush cannot be treated with neutrality by any serious Labour member. For all the talk of compassionate conservatism and nation-first policy from McCain, the choice of the **hard-Right** Sarah Palin as vice-presidential candidate shows quite clearly where the battle lines are to be drawn.

Boris Johnson, of course, has been as on message as ever. The Guardian ran an article that was slightly less ambiguous that Gordon Brown's implied endorsement of Obama, with the headline **"Barak Obama gets Surprise Endorsement from Boris Johnson"**

"[Boris Johnson said] 'I was looking at him on the news and just thinking what an amazing moment this is... watching his speech in Berlin and thinking what a critical moment this is for America and for attitudes towards what they can achieve amongst the black community. If Barack Obama can do it, it will be the most fantastic boost, I think, for black people everywhere around the world...

'I think [Republican candidate] John McCain has many, many wonderful qualities... but I think a Barack Obama victory would do fantastic things for the confidence and the feelings of black people around the world - that they can win.'

Asked if he endorsed Obama, he said: 'Yes.'"[6]

Boris aside, even William Hague seems to have a bit of a short memory, even with regard to the current US election. The Daily Torygraph told us earlier this year that:

"David Cameron has also expressed his admiration for Mr Obama and in an interview with the Telegraph Mr Hague calls him 'an exciting candidate'"[7]

The same article proudly declares the Republicans as the Conservatives' **sister party** although admits that:

"Mr Hague says that he has been making inroads with the potential decision-makers of a future Democrat regime in the White House. He said: 'I've been steadily extending our contacts with Democratic policy makers while the election has been going on'"[8]

British socialists (indeed, British conservatives) should, indeed, keep their noses out of the affairs of any independent country (not always advice followed by our American cousins...) But it is politically naïve (who are we kidding- it was a bit of silly and ill-thought out opportunism) to suggest that Gordon, or any person interested in politics should not form an opinion about the outcome of an election for the most powerful position on the planet.

Every Labour, Lib Dem, Green and, indeed, every progressive Tory in Britain will be crossing their fingers for one result:

Obama/Biden 2008.

Wednesday, 29 October 2008
Next US President: John McCain ?

Like any politically aware person on the planet at the moment, I have been assiduously following the election for the US President. Curiously, I keep getting this odd flashback to **April 1992**.

1992 was the first British General Election that I followed properly- as an idealist 14 year old, I waited to see the back of the hated (at least in my household) Thatcher government, now under its grey and uninspiring caretaker-leader John Major. At Labour press conferences, the front bench were introduced as "..the next Home Secretary…" and so on. **Neil Kinnock** was to be the next Prime Minster, and was feted by supporters like Stephen Fry, Anthony Sher and Sir Richard Attenborough in a party political broadcast entirely comprised of celebrity endorsements (the so-called "Luvvies for Labour" broadcast) A massive triumphant rally in **Sheffield** a few days before the poll continued to celebrate this impending victory.

On April 9th, in a record turnout, John Major's Tories received **more votes than any other party in history**- beating the record set by Labour's Clement Attlee in 1951 *(an election that Labour lost, owing to the oddities of the constituency system.)* **Even the pollsters were baffled**.

The BBC **called the election for Labour** at 10.00pm on April 9th, based on the most sophisticated exit poll they had ever conducted: voters were asked to cast a secret ballot for the pollsters after they had left the official polling station. This confirmed that the best result possible for the Tories was 3 short of a majority, and the best for Labour was a comfortable overall majority. **The result saw Major 20 seats ahead of combined rivals.**

(Incidentally, Eastbourne was a noteworthy result- the Tories took it with an **overall majority**, reversing the by-election gain by the Lib Dems less than two years before, which swept **David "whoops-there-goes-my-football-club" Bellotti** briefly into Westminster. All of the other by-election gains by Labour and the Lib Dems also returned to the Tories.)

In 1992, being a Tory was not trendy or even popular. So much so, that people were unwilling to **admit that they had voted Tory again**. Some purged their conscience by "voting" Labour in the exit poll, and hoping that no-one would find out. Many more, we can assume, **declined the offer to take part in the opinion poll process**.

Which brings us to America. The surge of grass roots support for Obama has made him the clear favourite: he whips up adoring crowds, he has an oratory comparable to JFK, he looks and sounds like the future. He has even won endorsements from traditional right wing figures like Colin Powell (and Boris Johnson)

Has this swung the tide ? Or have we simply repeated the UK's 1992 effect, where the republicans go to ground, and keep their voting intention quiet. All of the polls (indeed, both campaigns) are heavily focusing on the "Don't Know" voters. Is this huge group (representing millions of people) really made up of voters poring over the papers every day and agonising over the issues ? **Or does it contain a significant proportion of voters who don't want anyone to know they are a secret McCain/Palin fan**?

Never underestimate the Right. The Republicans continue to secure the backing of the hard Right, and, indeed the plain racist, as shown on last night's ITN News at Ten. **Trevor McDonald** experienced a radio phone in, when one woman explained about Obama being a Muslim. When McDonald points out that Obama is a practicing Christian, she assures him: *"No sir, he's a Muslim"*. In the same report, McDonald meets a Republican campaigner who points out to him: *"Barack Hussein Obama... it's not a normal American name..."*[9]

The **race card** is an ugly tactic in any society's politics, and I hope that an Obama victory consigns it to the dustbin, at least in the USA. But, as Trevor McDonald's report showed, and any grass roots campaigner in Britain will tell you, it is underestimated at your peril. With some elements even introducing a tenuously evidenced but potentially damaging strand of **Islampohobia** into the US election, race and culture remains off limits only amongst the official campaigns.

Like every Labour supporter in the country, and virtually everyone on the centre and Left across the globe, we cross our fingers tightly that the USA will elect Barak Obama, and open up, in so many ways, a **new chapter in world history**. However, as Obama attends rallies several times a day that make the Sheffield Rally look like a wake, we should all remember that it is not over until every vote has been won: and **the result is far from a foregone conclusion**.

Monday, 3 November 2008
24 Hours

...until the first projections roll in from the US. Not many of us political animals will get much sleep tomorrow night. I went to bed happy early in 2000, when the networks "called" Florida for Al Gore. I'm not making that mistake again.

Newsnight has just featured a panel of four eminent American commentators, including John McCain's former campaign manager. All were pointing out how remote McCain's road to the White House looks. One (and I wasn't taking names) suggested that, based on the polls, McCain would need to take ***"all of the 'don't knows' and that has never happened in history..."***

I'd like to feel optimistic, but **my gut reaction hasn't changed**. I still think that there is a significant conservative undercurrent: that many of the 'don't knows' are actually going to go out and vote McCain/Palin. Very possibly enough to pull off the shock of the century so far. **It's going to be mighty close !**

Monday, 10 November 2008
The day that the world changed

I like being wrong. Especially when the result is a seismic change such as **the election of Barack Obama**. I stayed up far too late watching the results being called (an interesting phenomenon in US politics: the TV network's exit polls are accepted as the result. In Britain, we learned not to do this after 1992...) But it was the following morning that really hit home.

A tearful **Jesse Jackson**, hailing the beginning of a new era. Jackson, the veteran of the Civil Rights movement, a man that knew **Martin Luther King**, now witnessing the election of America's first Black president.

My parents' generation remembered the sea-change of **Jack Kennedy's** election in 1960, by a far more slender margin (in my defence, Obama's win was not officially a "landslide": American psephologists define this as a margin of 55%:45% or more) Our generation will remember this week as a **defining moment** in their lives. **A day that the world changed forever.**

Friday, 15 August 2008
A worthy host for the Olympics ?

[A late addition to this chapter. I thought that in the interests of balance I should find an article from the columns that was complimentary about George W. Bush. And, believe it or not, I found one !]

China was not a universally popular choice for hosting the 2008 Olympic Games. At the time many people, quite rightly, highlighted the **human rights record** of the world's most populous country, ranging from the occupation of Tibet, to the high level of executions without due process, the imprisonment of political prisoners, the suppression of religion....

China, is, however, one of the most important economies in the world- not least in terms of consumer manufacturing: most British and American households would be pretty empty if all the Chinese furniture and electrical goods were removed ! The US had, therefore, to become China's new best friend in order to keep the markets open !   Which is why I was pleasantly surprised that George W. Bush was able to speak out on human rights concerns[1] on the eve of the games.

> *"The US believes the people of China deserve the fundamental liberty that is the natural right of all human beings... America stands in firm opposition to China's detention of political dissidents, human rights advocates and religious activists,"*[3]

China, of course, dismisses any such criticism as interfering in their "internal affairs". It cannot, however, avoid the fact that as part of its highly controversial, but successful bid to be awarded the games, it made promises on human rights, media freedoms and access to health and education, that seem to have been mysteriously forgotten.

If ever an opening ceremony became a **metaphor** for China's shortcomings, this was it. The footage of spectacular downtown fireworks shown round the world turned out to have been touched up- some were completely computer generated; and the little girl "singing" in the opening ceremony turned out to be miming: as the girl with the best voice, Yang Peiyi, was judged to be - and I quote:- ***"not as flawless"*** as the pretty little girl we saw on our screens.[4]

Many of us remember **Tiananmen Square** only too vividly. Things may have improved, but China still has a long way to travel on the human rights road before it truly deserves the international acclaim that it has (temporarily) won in these Olympics.

THE POLITICAL: THE PERSONAL

In amongst writing about politics, education and Eastbourne, I have occasionally allowed myself to insert a bit of my personal life into the columns. The death of a family member at 100, the death of a political friend who gave so much service- Ann Ring- were two such occasions. Hitting the ripe old age of 30 could not avoid a mention, and my two New Year round ups mixed the political and the personal. It's the end of the book- indulge me !

Sunday 23 December 2007
RIP: Ann Ring

Eastbourne Labour Party finds itself in mourning for one of its most dedicated, principled and unwavering supporters, Hampden Park campaigner Ann Ring, who died in November after a typically spirited (and always optimistic and good- humoured) battle against cancer.

Ann was the stalwart of the Hampden Park Labour Party branch, of which she was a member for more than 30 years, along with her late husband Brian. There was not a leaflet through a door in Hampden Park that Ann had not helped deliver, and not a single campaign run by the local Party that did not owe its existence to Ann's tireless fundraising. Coffee Mornings, Jumble Sales and the monthly 50% draw all owed their success to Ann's hard work. (I joked with a Labour colleague about what Ann would have said at her own funeral- "All these people here, why haven't we got a raffle?")

Ann was not just a fundraiser: she was a committed and practical socialist. Always on the left of the Party, her loyalty to the Party never wavered, although like most of us she had her sharp words for government policy in private!

In recent years, she stood for Labour in the local elections, and on two occasions I had the privilege of being her running mate in multi-candidate elections in Hampden Park. It was during her last election campaign in May 2007 that she was diagnosed with cancer.

Ann was not just a political activist, she was a genuine community campaigner. She was vice-chairman of the Hampden Park Community Association, running the lunch club. For many years she was treasurer of the Scout and Guide hut; she was a regular worshipper and helper at St Peter's Church, and was active in the original Hampden Park Post Office campaign- to save (unsuccessfully) the Queens Parade office.

A committed trades unionist like Brian, she kept her troops marshaled for the GMB in the ETC kitchens until her retirement, and had just started her retirement programme of seeing the world when she became ill.

Ann's funeral was packed- people standing not just in the aisles but in the foyer to pay their respects. Her daughter Pauline gave a heartfelt eulogy for her mother- finishing by reflecting that Ann had been sad that she could not do more for her young grandchildren. Pauline replied "If they can be brought up with your values, then you will have given them everything."

The way we were- a fundraiser at Ann's house with the Labour faithful. Back row l-r: Clive Wallis, Dave Brinson, Colin Wainwright, Brian Ring, Letta Page. Front row: Terry Page, Gill Roles, Jon Pettigrew, Troy Tester and Ann Ring.

Saturday, 29 December 2007
...and I'll cry if I want to

Aaaargh ! It's finally happened! 30 has crept stealthily up behind me, and my twenties have disappeared, never to return!

Oh well, the birthday cake might make up for it.

It left me to look back over the last decade, and where I've come in that time, and surely I'm allowed to be a bit self indulgent on my 30th birthday and write about me ! A few thoughts:

10 years ago, I was a young and idealistic student, completing my degree, and moving in the heady world of Middlesex University politics. Shortly afterwards, I began my training in losing elections, by failing to win the Presidency of Middlesex University Students Union. (I console myself that, as a member of a 200-student campus, I had an uphill struggle in the recognition stakes against the eventual winner, a student at the 5,000+ business campus in Hendon.)

10 years ago, my income was derived from pulling pints in the Greyhound Pub in term time, and selling deckchairs on Eastbourne Seafront in the summer. Over the next ten years, they have been replaced by an intermittent (and totally unprofitable) acting career, working in shops, doing the books for a double glazing company (no...I didn't sell it, don't worry), working for a market research company, a costume jewellery supplier, and enumerating for the 2001 census (which technically made me a civil servant for a couple of months...) Finally, in 2002, I returned to the classroom to train as a teacher, ending up at Ratton School, where I remain.

It was a mere 8 years ago that I fought my first election as a Labour candidate, fighting the Willingdon ward for Wealden District Council. I moved across the border the following year, to come in fourth in Ratton Ward (thanks, Theresia Williamson!) and then in 2001 I stood in Hampden Park, polling 996 votes and a good second place. I fought Hampden Park a further 5 times, last year alongside my good friend, the much missed Ann Ring.

During those ten years, Britain has gained its first ever National Minimum Wage (opposed by the last Tory government, who called it "immoral") the first ever right for paid holidays from work (no compulsory holiday time at all under the Tories.) We've seen protection at work for part-timers, working parents, older workers, and equality for lesbians and gay men (much to the chagrin of Nigel Waterson who opposed every single piece of LGB equality)

The international situation has also changed in that time- not least the threat posed by terrorism- I remember vividly working in a local primary school on September 11th 2001, and realising as we listened to the radio that, in so many ways, the world changed forever that day.

So what beckons for the next ten years? Can Gordon Brown equal the record of his "closest political friend" (or nemesis, depending on who you believe) Tony Blair? I shall be playing my small part in pursuit of that goal, when Gordon goes to the Palace, and I throw myself on the mercy of the Eastbourne voter? Will I still be writing this blog when I'm 40? Will there be such a thing? Watch this space on 29th December 2017 for the definitive answer.....

Monday, 31 December 2007
Another year over

So, that was 2007. The end of the Tory council in Eastbourne and the beginning of a guaranteed 4 years of the Lib Dems. Also the end of my 20's (I don't know which of those two fills me with more apprehension…) Nationally, the end of the Blair years and the beginning of the Brown era, and the general election that never was.

Pretty much every political blogger in the land is going to do their take on the national events of 2007, and I don't want to clog up the blogsphere with my thoughts- so I'll restrict myself to a few Eastbourne observations:-

Biggest local surprise: The end (????) of Pay to Park
The May elections were dominated by this issue- a Tory County Council imposing a pay to park scheme. The Lib Dems said they'd stop it if they won the Borough elections, and after a lot of posturing from both sides, the pay to park scheme was replaced for the time being by an "interim" scheme of enforcement without charges, while legal wrangles are sorted out. The Lib Dems were cock-a-hoop, but this issue is still far from settled, and will be a ticking time bomb that is certain to go off sometime in 2008.

Biggest electoral surprise: The Tories lose Upperton.
Upperton ward has always been true-blue, with one 4 year gap in the mid-1990's, when the Lib Dems defeated the late George Mills after a deeply personal and nasty attack on this decent man, as a "Hampden Park Reject". No such opportunities this year, you would have thought, with veteran Ann Murray and former deputy leader of the council Bob Lacey. However, in one that you really didn't see coming, the Lib Dems took two seats this ward, and nearly ousted the popular former Mayor and leader of the council Graham Marsden as well. Always good for democracy to see that supposedly "safe" seat can change hands (even if you don't particularly care for the replacements!)

Biggest local disappointment: DGH to lose maternity
The decision we all feared- the PCT deciding to close consultant-led maternity at the DGH, despite the efforts of local cross-party campaigners, Eastbourne GPs, and the overwhelming majority of local residents. There is the possibility of a judicial review in the new year. But surely the Secretary of State can find the political will to overrule the arrogant and out of touch PCT leadership (who covered themselves in glory at the public meeting by setting their private security heavies on the Bishop of Lewes!)

Favourite local news story: Waterson and the gay community
OK, it was one of mine (that's why I liked it !), at the time that "Dave" Cameron was cosying up to every community that the Tories had shafted when in power. His warm support for the lesbian and gay community and civil partnerships gave me a chance to dig up a few morsels from Nigel Waterson's past on this issue.

Second place in the category goes to the Lloyd won't turn Tory story, where Stephen Lloyd ruled out taking part in any Tory-Lib Dem coalition in Westminster. Now his new party leader is thrusting right-wing former Leon Brittain speechwriter Nick Clegg, (if it looks like a Tory, and quacks like a Tory….) could my "kite flying" end up being strangely prophetic? Read the full article, (with a pretty good put down about Lloyd's lefty past by Nigel Waterson, I have to admit)[1]

Best Savaging-from-a-Dead-Sheep: Ian Lucas' Blog
The sheep comment was coined by Denis Healey of Geoffrey Howe, and comes in handy again in response to the honour of making the headline (really !) on Ian Lucas' blog: "Labour's Dave Brinson: Nice Bloke, Rubbish Blogger". Basically, in November, I took a sabbatical from writing this blog for a few weeks- for a number of personal reasons. Determined to keep on top of my work responsibilities (including my duty to the NUT members I support and help across East Sussex,) I thought it would be honest to say "Look, I'm taking a break" rather than scratch around and post occasional quick or badly researched stuff to fill the void. Surely this in itself wasn't a newsworthy item ? Apparently it was. On the other hand, it does mean I can use the quote "Dave Brinson: 'Nice Bloke' says ex-Tory leader," on future leaflets… (Second place goes to the anonymous right winger, who, in October, called me a "socialist pig dog" for spelling former PM Sir Alec Douglas-Home's name...er...correctly...)

Saddest Loss: Ann Ring: My friend, running-mate, chief fundraiser, committed socialist and a champion of the community in Hampden Park for more than 40 years. One of the most decent people I have had the pleasure of knowing. If you didn't know Ann, read the post of 23rd December.

So, what has 2008 got in store ? Certainly a year of challenges- and I'm looking forward to them immensely!

Happy New Year !

Monday, 20 October 2008
RIP Nan, an eyewitness to a century

One of the reasons for my recent absence from the blogsphere has been the recent passing of my **grandmother Dorothy Brinson**, at the magnificent age of 100.

Dorothy was an important person throughout my childhood, living just a few doors down, and was lucky enough to remain in her own home, and relatively independent until just a year ago, when she moved to the care of Elstree Court in Meads.

I am grateful for all of the kind words and support from colleagues and friends at this time. It **doesn't seem quite right to publish a family obituary on a political blog**, but it did get me thinking about the massive changes that my grandmother saw in her long life.

Dorothy was 5 years old at the outbreak of World War 1, and the "Great War" would have provided the background to her early childhood. She would have seen the many men who returned, wounded and invalided to the land fit for heroes, and the women, only a few years older than her, who would never find a husband.

Dorothy left school at 14, even though she was doing well and had wanted to complete her studies. As the eldest daughter, she was expected to **go out to work and help her mother**. She often told us of how she had to catch the 6.00am workman's train into the city. During her lifetime, she saw school leaving ages rise to 15, then 16. Dorothy and her husband (John, who she married in 1933) brought up three children during the second world war- and she would have experienced the fear of having her husband serving in the RAF, and the stresses of being evacuated with her children to the far North of England.

After the war, Dorothy started work as a school secretary: a job she remained in until 67. Widowed tragically early in 1964, she took on the role of solo householder with some gusto, and developed a skill for DIY, doing her own painting and decorating well into her 80's: the spirit of the WWII generation clearly being something that didn't diminish with age.

The **birth of the NHS** and the pledge of cradle-to-grave welfare was a symbol of the determination never to return to the sickness and poverty of the pre-war years. Dorothy saw many developments in the health system. The death of her father under a general anaesthetic in 1927 left her with a fear of operations: in her 90's she experienced what once would have been unthinkable- the fitting of a heart pacemaker, and the removal of a cataract, **both under a local anaesthetic.** She was back at home in her own armchair just an hour after the cataract op.

In 1973, Dorothy was left some money, and was able to **fly to Australia** to visit her brother and his children who had emigrated there in the 1960's. This was a major event at the time- she was thrown a "Good luck" party by her colleagues at work. Nowadays, international air travel is commonplace (perhaps too much so...?) As a child, Dorothy and her brother delighted in plugging earphones into the "cats whiskers" radio (powered by an acid-filled accumulator battery) Her lifetime saw the invention of the telephone, the TV (black and white first !) the tape and CD player, the microwave, and many other inventions that became part of her everyday life.

Dorothy lived through **19 Prime Ministers**, and saw many political changes, including the first Labour government. She married John Brinson who was a Labour man, and whose brother Bill was Mayor of Poplar in the 1950's. She was a fan of politicians like Shirley Williams and David Steel, although loved to listen to people as diverse as Tony Benn and Ted Heath. She identified Tony Blair as a rising star even back in Neil Kinnock's time.

Never a member of the Labour Party, she nonetheless did her bit in recent elections: in 1997 she had to be firmly taken home after spending hours **taking numbers for Labour** at the polling stations both in Willingdon, and the town hall, and also offered her house as a committee room during local elections. I well recall her checking off numbers "bingo style" on paper Reading pads, with the late Russ Fisher and Terry Page (no computer being allowed in!)

RIP, Dorothy Brinson: a remarkable life, and an eyewitness to a century of social history.

Monday, 12 January 2009
What was great in 2008 ?

What was great in 2008 ?
As Private Eye's favourite poet, EJ Thribb may have put it... "So, Farewell then, 2008" Another year over, and an opportunity to look back at the highs and lows of those 365 days....

THE HIGHS....

<u>**Obama in the White House:**</u> It's not often that I cry in front of the TV, but the morning after the US Presidential election was one of them. Not just as we now had clear, tangible evidence of the end of the **George W. Bush** era, but a figure who (regardless of colour, incidentally) projected a message of **hope and compassion** for the world. My Tory friend Ian Lucas, who was rooting for John McCain, cautioned in his Herald column that Obama had "the most liberal voting record in the Senate."

Hooray.

For the last 20 years, American politicians have avoided the **"L" word** and tried to project themselves as **small-c conservative**. "Out" liberals in the States have to constantly struggle against the right-wing media, the conservative=patriotic mantra, the political organisations associated with the "religious right" and the "moral majority" (I **don't** include the churches themselves in this, by the way, in America just as in the rest of the world, people of faith come from many different viewpoints and convictions) Now, **liberal is no longer a dirty word in America** (nor, we hope, is internationalist) A new dawn for America ?

"Yes we can…"

<u>**Saved the DGH:**</u> A victory for common sense- after a genuinely cross-party, cross-Eastbourne campaign, consultant led maternity services were finally saved at the DGH. **Liz Walke** quite rightly and deservedly received the Freedom of the Borough in recognition of her work: congratulations too to all of those who lobbied, marched and fundraised to keep the campaign going. **Special hats-off to Labour's representative on the committee, Richard Goude**.

<u>**Cracking the NUT:**</u> On a personal level, being elected to the National Executive of my union, the **National Union of Teachers** was pretty special.

A bit of a baptism of fire, as, within a few weeks we were embroiled in our first strike action for 22 years, but there's a lot more to the job than that: and it has been a challenge I've relished.

THE LOWS...

The economy: The days of those posters of Major and Lamont as the **Laurel and Hardy of British politics** seem a long time ago. Mr Boom and Mr Bust doesn't work as a Tory-bashing insult any more. So long ago it seems, that we forget the image of the **boy Cameron** carrying Norman Lamont's bags in the background on Black Wednesday.

We thought that the ten years of quarter-upon-quarter growth would go on forever, but the world economy has put an end to the economic dream. But, the indications are that Brown may still be able to lead us out.

It was **not Gordon Brown's doing** that Fannie May and Freddie Mac (the two major US mortgage underwriters) got into trouble. It was **not Gordon Brown's doing** that the toxic sub-prime mortgage market in the States impacted around the world. It **is not Gordon's fault** that even the unstoppable Chinese economy is in marked slowdown.

As the downturn started to bite, Labour's poll rating started to increase. Gordon seemed to have, pardon the pun, money in the bank with the electorate when it came to economic competence. There was a feeling among many that these were times for a man who knew what he was talking about. So will the action be enough ?

Recapitalising the banks- recognised as necessary, and a model being followed across the world. *TIME* magazine had Gordon in their annual "People Who Mattered" feature- noting:

"His recapitalisation scheme for British banks unveiled in October, quickly became the model for other countries' rescue efforts and inspired the recalibration of the US plan"[3]

The VAT cut didn't exactly get my pulse racing, and calls to hold down the **minimum wage** even less so (although that will depend on what happens to wages across the rest of the economy, so hold fire for a moment, Dave...) Equally, the recognition that those on super-incomes of £150,000+ should pay more tax was welcome, although it won't come until 2011, **when, in fact, we should have done it in 1997.**

This will be the story to watch in the countdown to the next election. For all the glamour, for all the personality politics and glib soundbites, the message of Clinton's 1992 victory is paramount:
"It's the economy, stupid !"

The end of Eastbourne Buses: It was Britain's **first and oldest municipal bus company**. It had remained the property of the people of Eastbourne for over 100 years, surviving recession, downturn, the rise of car ownership and the rabid privatisations of the Thatcher era. But it **couldn't survive the Lib Dems in the Town Hall**. Our bus company- rightly identified by Nigel Waterson (of all people) as part of the "family silver" has gone. **Forever.** If I want to take a bus in Eastbourne, I will now be contributing to the profits of transport behemoth Stagecoach, run by Scotland's most active and prominent homophobe, Brian Souter. Frankly, I think I might walk.

Airbourne: The decision to **charge** for the erstwhile "biggest free airshow in the country" was typical Lib Dem madness. Not only did it deter visitors, and alienate the local council tax payers who had always underwritten the show, it became a **catalogue of disasters**.

The council "didn't realise" that the police would charge to cover a profit-making event, nor did they seem to calculate the huge cost of fencing off the seafront, or employing ticketing companies. An additional £250,000 was quoted by the Eastbourne Herald, adding to a final **loss of more than £360,000 to the local council taxpayer**. And, as I pointed out in the Herald, they repeatedly put **Norman Kinnish** (a non-political employee, directed by the politicians) to carry the can for the political decisions made by David Tutt and co. Not just incompetent, but cowardly, too.

Bye bye, Nan: As readers will know, I lost my Grandmother in September, which was a huge wrench. But, as I said in the article, 100 years can't be sniffed at- what a life: and witness to what a century of our history. I was privileged to know such an amazing woman for 30 years of my life.

Who knows what 2009 will bring....

AFTERWORD

When the former Tory leader of Eastbourne Borough Council, Ian Lucas posted an article on his own 'blog entitled "Dave Brinson: Nice bloke, rubbish blogger" I did consider whether it was time to stop- could I post regularly enough to keep the column readable ?

By 2009, it was clear that I couldn't, so I called it a day. Interestingly, Ian Lucas also stopped blogging around the same time, although he still writes a very readable online column for the Eastbourne Herald once a week (I tend to disagree with nearly all of it...)

At the time of going to print, we are weeks away from a General Election, at which I will be flying the Labour flag in Eastbourne. I continue to serve on the National Executive of the NUT (to which I was re-elected this year), so it's fair to say I'm still being kept busy.

On the other hand- could the result of the General Election (whatever it is?) inspire me to put pen to paper (or rather finger to keyboard) once again? Who knows? Either way, it was fun writing this much, and I hope you enjoyed it.

                                                Dave Brinson
                                                March 2010

SOURCES

Chapter 1: Labour Days
1. Theyworkforyou.com
2. ePolitix: 23.9.07
3. Daily Telegraph 14.1.07
4. Eastbourne Gazette 18.3.08
5. iloveeastbourne.blogspot.co.uk
6. Livingstone, Ken "If Voting Changed Anything, They'd Abolish It"
7. lukeakehurst.blogspot .com
8. The Guardian, 15.9.08
9. From the Heart, Eastbourne Herald Online 22.9.08

Chapter 2: The Opposition
1. The Guardian 19.9.07
2. Press Association 22.7.07
3. The Guardian, 16.8.09 and www.labour.org.uk
4. www.bnp.org.uk
5. http://news.bbc.co.uk/
6. www.ashleymote.com 8.9.07
7. Daily Mirror 15.9.07
8. The Observer, 16.9.07
9. Daily Mirror 15.9.07
10. The Independent 19.9.05
11. Press Association. 13.1.08
12. Kevin Maguire in the New Statesman 29.5.06
13. iloveeastbourne.blogspot.com
14. Dominic Lawson in The Independent, 29.2.08
15. ePolitix.com 29.12.08
16. Daily Mail, 9.9.06

Chapter 3- Health
1. Eastbourne Herald, 13/7/07
2. Ibid
3. East Sussex Hospitals NHS Trust- Trust News December 2006
4. Eastbourne Herald 1.2.08
5. Daily Mail, 3.3.08
6. Eastbourne Herald 5.9.08

Chapter 4- Education,
1. Sky News, 15.2.08
2. NASUWT Press release 15.2.08
3. Daily Express 27.3.08
4. TheyWorkForYou.com
5. Times Online 14.5.08
6. Press Release, East Sussex NUT

Chapter 5- Equalities
1. Eastbourne Herald 15.6.07 and Press Release from Eastbourne Labour Party 11.6.07
2. www.eastbournetoday.co.uk
3. Ibid
4. Tatchell, Peter, The Battle For Bermondsey
5. ConservativeHome 6.6.07

Chapter 6- Airbourne
1. Various articles in the Eastbourne Herald and Gazette during August 2001.
2. From the Heart, Eastbourne Herald Online, 9.6.08
3. Eastbourne Herald, 12.6.08
4. Eastbourne Herald 5.9.09
5. Ibid

Chapter 7- Up the Workers
1. Eastbourne Herald 29.3.07
2. Tribune 3.8.07
3. ASDA Press Release, 4.10.06
4. Usdaw Press Release, 13.8.04
5. The Guardian, 20.10.08
6. Ibid

Chapter 8- Law and Liberty
1. Martin Rowson in Tribune,
2. O'Farrell, John, Thing Can Only Get Better
3. Politics.co.uk 10.6.08
4. Labour Party Members e-mail, 12.6.08

5. Eastbourne Herald, 17.10.08
6. BBC News 28.5.02
7. Ibid

Chapter 9- Arty Time
1. Sunday Telegraph 17.6.07
2. Ibid
3. Peter Hall, quoted by the Sheffield Theatres website
4. House of Commons Hansard,
5. Conservative Governments and Football Regulation Steve Greenfield & Guy Osborn, University of Westminster

Chapter 10- Transport
1. Eastbourne Herald 16.11.06
2. Eastbourne Herald, 17.8.07
3. House of Commons Hansard, 1.2.07

Chapter 11- International
1. Reuters, 28.12.07
2. BBC News Online, 18.3.08
3. BBC News 7.8.08
4. BBC News, 12.08.08
5. Associated Press 10.9.08
6. The Guardian, 1.8.08
7. Daily Telegraph 26.2.08
8. Ibid
9. ITV News at Ten, 28.10.08

Chapter 12- Personal
1. Eastbourne Herald 29.10.07
2. Iloveeastbourne.blogspot.com, November 2007
3. TIME Magazine, December 29th 2008,

www.ingramcontent.com/pod-product-compliance
Ingram Content Group UK Ltd.
Pitfield, Milton Keynes, MK11 3LW, UK
UKHW041437180426
11947UKWH00007B/499